GLORIOUS
SUMMER

The Sussex CCC Championship 2003

GLORIOUS SUMMER

The Sussex CCC Championship 2003

John Wallace

TEMPUS

Sussex squad 2003. From left to right, back row: S.H. Osborne (physiotherapist), J. Carmichael (physiotherapist), Carl Hopkinson, Billy Taylor, Shaun Rashid, Paul Hutchison, Keith Greenfield (academy director). Middle row: Mark Davis, Bas Zuiderent, Matt Prior, Tim Ambrose, Michael Yardy, Richard Montgomerie, Kevin Innes. Seated: Jason Lewry, Mushtaq Ahmed, Mark Robinson (First XI coach), James Kirtley (vice-captain), Chris Adams (captain), Robin Martin-Jenkins, Peter Moores (director of cricket), Murray Goodwin, Tony Cottey.

Frontispiece: Chris Adams proudly holds the Championship trophy.

First published 2004

Tempus Publishing Limited
The Mill, Brimscombe Port,
Stroud, Gloucestershire, GL5 2QG

© John Wallace, 2004

The right of John Wallace to be identified as the Author
of this work has been asserted in accordance with the
Copyrights, Designs and Patents Act 1988.

British Library Cataloguing in Publication Data.
A catalogue record for this book is available from the British Library.

ISBN 0 7524 3224 9

Typesetting and origination by Tempus Publishing Limited
Printed and bound in Great Britain

CONTENTS

FOREWORD

A glorious summer it certainly was, from the point of view of both the weather and the cricket. Sussex at long last are the County Champions. It may have taken over 100 years, but we've done it, and I am delighted to have been associated with the club as the 2003 president.

There have been some wonderful moments in my cricketing life, all unforgettable. The debut for England some fifty years ago in 1954, scoring a century in Trinidad to help England win the series against the mighty West Indies in 1960 and, shortly after in 1963, standing alongside Ted Dexter as he received the Gillette Cup in the very first year of competitive one-day cricket.

But as I stood on the players' balcony on 18 September last year and Sussex reached the magical figure of 300 in their first innings, all that went before was left way behind. That was the greatest moment, and I was delighted to have been in the middle of an interview for television just at the right time and to be able to convey the emotion of the scene to those viewing.

The association of the Parks family with Sussex spans some eighty years. My father first played for the county in 1923, my uncle Harry played until 1948 and I made my debut in 1949. The club came very close on three occasions in the early 1930s, and the team that I played in was second to Surrey in 1953 under the captaincy of David Sheppard, who was indeed the finest captain that I ever played under. The county came close under John Barclay's captaincy, but we were still kept waiting for another twenty years before Chris Adams and his team made history last September.

The 2003 season is now history, and how splendid that a book recording the matches that culminated in that magical moment on 18 September has now been written. All the facts are there, the little incidents that contribute to making a game a contest, along with the thoughts of players and spectators alike as they sweated over the final outcome. And there is a theme running through that the Sussex Championship win was due to a team effort, a great team performance that saw everyone who took part help to achieve the end result.

Now, as this book is published, Sussex start out on their quest to retain the title, and how wonderful it would be if this could happen. It is a good team, of that there can be no doubt, and will certainly be challenging, but whatever happens the aim must be to enjoy the game, both as players and spectators.

Jim Parks
President of Sussex County Cricket Club

PREFACE

It was Hitler, strangely enough, who saw to it that I became a Sussex supporter. I was born in South London and but for the events of 1939 I would almost certainly have attended Dulwich College and watched much of my cricket at The Oval. I would have been able to claim that I had been to the same school as Hugh Bartlett and Billy Griffith, but instead my family, once evacuated to West Sussex, decided to stay there and I was enrolled at Collyer's School, Horsham, the *alma mater* of George Cox junior and Paul Parker. A fair swap, I suspect, especially when it comes to fielding!

When cricket resumed in 1946 I was Sussex bred, if not born. There was clearly only one county for me. I delighted in a James Langridge century against Worcestershire in the first match of the season, but was saddened, although by no means despondent, when Sussex finished bottom of the Championship. Better things would follow, I was sure. In the late forties and early fifties it was not unusual for me to cycle the twenty or so miles from West Chiltington to Hove or, if I was lazy, catch the number 22 bus and then walk up Holland Road to the ground. The performances of the Langridge brothers, of George Cox, Charlie Oakes and Harry Parks were the things that filled me with awe, although there were times when counties such as Middlesex, containing such heroes as Denis Compton and Bill Edrich, appeared to sweep Sussex away.

Before I left for university in 1950 I had, of course, sampled village cricket in Sussex. Before I got a game for the local side I scored, as lads have to – even, I recall, at Priory Park, Chichester – and then, once in the team, I played on many grounds in West Sussex, not least the Manor Ground at Worthing. Even though I had effectively ceased to live in Sussex from the age of eighteen – university at Southampton, an RAF commission served mainly in Wiltshire and teaching posts in Guildford and Tunbridge Wells – my thoughts were never far from Sussex cricket in the summer months. Even when I was living for a year in Bavaria I would always go the local station to buy a tissue-thin copy of the continental *Daily Telegraph* to find out how David Sheppard *et al* were managing, or in later years when I was abroad I would never fail to visit the local library to consult copies of *The Times* that had come out while I had been away. I believe that I can claim in all honesty never to have failed to read the Sussex scoresheet for every day of every match since 1946.

I have lived in Tunbridge Wells for the past thirty-seven years, but it has its advantages – people claim that from here you can hit balls from Kent into Sussex and I can recall even now being told, when I was stumped in a local match, that I was so far down that I was halfway to Frant! What better thing can there be than moving towards a Sussex village?

My career, of course, afforded me little time to watch Sussex, but since just before my retirement I have become a Sussex member and have watched the County and enjoyed writing three books about its fortunes. The 2003 season was, however, quite special for me, as for many others. I sat there at Hove on that pleasant September afternoon and when Murray Goodwin pulled the ball to the boundary, which meant that no team could now catch Sussex, I stood up and clapped, as all the other spectators did so politely – no high-fives, no unseemly clamour of triumphalism, but just quiet applause. As the loudspeakers played *Sussex by the Sea* and the team did their laps of honour I must confess to just a slight frisson of emotion when I understood what had finally happened. It won't be as exciting when they do it again in 2004!

BIBLIOGRAPHY

John Barclay, *The Appeal of the Championship* (Fairfield Books)
Nicholas Sharp, *Sussex – Seven times the Bridesmaid*

C&G Cricket Year 2003 (edited by Jonathan Agnew) (Bloomsbury)
Playfair Cricket Annual (relevant editions)
The Cricketer
The Wisden Cricket Monthly
The Wisden Cricketer
The Daily Telegraph
The Times
The Independent
The Guardian
The Argus
The Kent and Sussex Courier
Wisden Cricketers' Almanack (relevant editions)

ACKNOWLEDGEMENTS

I should like to thank Jim Parks, president of Sussex County Cricket Club, for finding the time to write an excellent foreword to this book. I am most grateful, as ever, to Roger Packham for his reading of the text and the host of useful suggestions and amendments that he has made, and to Cara Minns and Richard Taylor of *The Argus* for their kind gesture of support with some of the photographs.

I am particularly indebted, for their ready help with photographs, to Lindsay Vass and Angela Moore, but I also tender thanks to Sally Taylor of *The Kent and Sussex Courier*, John Dawson, Roger Ockenden, Neil Fisher and, last but certainly not least, to Nicholas Sharp for the loan of items from his magnificent collection.

As ever, I owe a debt to Rob Boddie of the Sussex CCC library, whose constant interest and encouragement and the loan of useful items has been invaluable, to James Howarth of Tempus Publishing, to Chris White for his suggestions on the use of English, to John and Paul Fowling for their expert help with proof-reading and, of course, to my wife Anne for her understanding of my desire to write books on Sussex cricket.

INTRODUCTION: YEARS OF ENDEAVOUR

WHY DID IT ALL TAKE SO LONG?

Being first has not been a frequent occurrence in the history of Sussex cricket. While it is true that George Langdon, Sussex's secretary in 1839, organised the first county club in the country, that James Lillywhite was England's first Test captain when he led his side against Australia in March 1877 and that the County were the initial winners of the inaugural one-day trophy, the Gillette Cup, in September 1963, there have been, sadly, rather more troughs than peaks in the course of Sussex's 164-year cricketing history. It's all rather strange because an all-time Sussex XI could surely do battle with the best. Ranji and Fry, Duleep and Sheppard, Dexter and Parks, not to mention Greig, were in their day among the most entertaining batsmen in the world, even though some have argued that Sussex has at times had a fundamental weakness in bowling. Had the critics perhaps forgotten that Tate in the 1920s was the best in the world, that Snow and Imran managed to capture the odd scalp and that Mushtaq has now provided the County with a world-class spinner?

For most aficionados, however, especially among what might be termed the older brigade, acknowledging as they do the raffish brilliance of almost forgotten 'golden ages' and the one-day triumphs, there has been only one competition really worth winning and that is the County Championship. Few dreamed that Sussex would ever pull it off. *The Times* leader termed it so aptly: *'The longest delay waiting padded-up in the pavilion'*. It was not perhaps a lack of faith, nor a failure of interest, but simply the fact that such a lengthy period without success had elapsed since the County's foundation. Meanwhile a seemingly upstart county like Glamorgan – goodness, they did not enter the ranks of the first class until 1921! – had already pocketed the trophy three times and near-neighbours such as Surrey, Kent and Hampshire had all been winners – the first-named on more occasions than a Sussex man would wish to recall. Yet, miraculously to some, more evidently to others (like Tony Pigott, the chief executive after the 1997 'revolution'), the last match of the 2003 season saw the trophy raised aloft by Chris Adams, not a Sussex man by birth but one who has espoused the County's fortunes just as closely as those born and bred in the South Saxon County. A vignette to note, perhaps: Tony Pigott, when questioned in 1997 by a member of a certain age, about the County's chances under his new regime, replied, just a little harshly: 'Sussex will lift the Championship before you die.' His own stewardship died quite quickly, but he was right about one thing. The gentleman didn't die and was there at Hove on 18 September to see Murray Goodwin pull Phillip DeFreitas to the midwicket boundary close to the pavilion, and the score move from 298 to 302, securing the 6th point needed to put Sussex firmly beyond the grasp of the other seventeen counties.

It might be instructive to wonder why it took Sussex 164 years to lift the title. One answer is quite simple: perhaps it did not take that time at all. Peter Wynne-Thomas, cricket statistician extraordinary and honorary secretary of the Association of Cricket Statisticians, has produced a chart, not wholly complete, it is true, covering the years 1826-1863, which shows six 'Championships' for Sussex plus one shared with Nottinghamshire. While it is a fact that Sussex were known to be strong enough to take on the England team in the 1820s and 1830s, this is all rather outline material. In 1864, however, the year John Wisden of Sussex started his famous almanack, a few counties started a somewhat more structured Championship, but it was not until 1872–73, after the leading nine counties – Surrey, Nottinghamshire, Middlesex, Yorkshire, Kent, Sussex, Gloucestershire, Lancashire and Derbyshire – had met in Hanover Street, London, and then at The Oval, that a better set of rules for the Championship was determined. In 1873, the year after Sussex moved from their Brunswick ground to the site in Eaton Road, Hove, which they have now occupied for the past 131 seasons, the revised County Championship began.

Between 1873 and 1889 Sussex's performance amongst the nine counties was wholly unspectacular: bottom in seven seasons, 8th in five more and in one season alone, that of 1875, was there anything to crow about. George Washer, once an indefatigable Sussex scorer and statistician boldly places the County in equal 1st place for 1875 in his *Complete Record of Sussex County Cricket*. On the other hand, the more dispassionate Bill Frindall in his *Wisden Book of Cricket Records* shows six sources, including *Wisden* and both the *Green* and the *Red Lillywhite* (none of these could have been more pro-Sussex!), which award the title clearly to Nottinghamshire. Rowland Bowen, in a fascinating article in the 1959 edition of *Wisden* entitled 'The Early County Champions' argues strongly that Sussex had no claim at all on the title. He cites the fact that none of the contemporary sources did other than to declare Nottinghamshire Champions and adds that it was not until 1958, when Washer published his book, that Sussex ever claimed the title. Although there were some very odd ways of determining Champions in those olden days – 'fewest matches lost' was one – the fact is that Nottinghamshire won six, drew three and lost one, while Sussex won five, drew one and lost two. Sussex did, however, do quite well: they beat Kent by ten wickets at Catford Bridge when Richard Fillery took seven for 24, Gloucestershire by seven wickets at Hove and Hampshire at St Cross, Winchester, by an innings and 27 runs. Returning to Hove they overcame Kent by an innings and 266 runs as the Sussex total reached 414 (their highest up to that point in county cricket) and their captain, Joseph Cotterill, reached 191, the highest score of the season. Sadly, in the return match at Hove with Hampshire (not numbered among the strongest sides at that time) they went down by 28 runs, although James Lillywhite junior and Richard Fillery, with ten wickets each, bowled unchanged throughout the visitors' two innings. This loss might well have cost them the Championship, although Roy Webber, who in 1957 first raised the possibility of Sussex's having jointly won the Championship in 1875, has pointed out that Hampshire may well have not been regarded as among the 'real' counties at that stage. Sussex's defeat, therefore, may not have been counted among the losses, so on the 'fewest matches lost' principle they might have been seen to share the title with Nottinghamshire and Lancashire.

Sussex went on to draw with Surrey at The Oval and then to beat them by an innings and 37 runs at Hove, only to record a second loss at Cheltenham when Gloucestershire triumphed by 40 runs. Perhaps predictably, the *History of Yorkshire County Cricket* awards

J.M. Cotterill, Sussex captain in 1875.

2nd place to their county in 1875, which is perhaps unfair, but, on balance and the evidence available, it seems that Sussex were probably not 1st or even equal 1st.

The Championship continued in a somewhat unsatisfactory form until 1887 when there was another meeting, this time at Lord's under the chairmanship of Lord Harris. Delegates from thirteen clubs met to investigate the setting up of a County Cricket Council to assist the MCC with the management of the game. In the 1880s Sussex had continued to fare badly, although they had in the short-lived Frederick Lucas from Warnham a wholly outstanding batsman, while Billy Newham, George Brann, Walter Humphreys and George Bean were all cricketers of merit. The council, formed as a result of the 1887 meeting, came up with a revised plan for the first-class cricketing counties, which took effect from the 1890 season. This is now generally regarded as the start of the County Championship as it is known today, so Sussex perhaps did not need 164 but a mere 113 years to record their first win!

The 1890s did not produce significantly better results for Sussex, but it was perhaps the period when the seeds of greater things were sown. In 1893 the County acquired the services of Billy Murdoch, the thirty-eight-year-old Victoria and Australia batsman and a great friend of Dr W.G. Grace, who immediately took over the captaincy. He was a player of some pedigree who had played for Australia in the second match of the initial Test series in 1877 and had captained his country between 1880 and 1884, among other feats scoring 286 for the Australian tourists against Sussex at Hove in 1882. He then gave up cricket for a time and settled in England, only to reappear as Australian captain in the 1890 series in England. In the winter of 1891/92 he toured South Africa with W.W. Read's side and even played for England at Cape Town in March 1892! Staying in England, he transferred his interest to Sussex from 1893. One year later he was joined in the Sussex ranks by Charles Fry and in 1895 Ranjitsinhji came to Hove.

Three very formidable amateur batsmen now formed the core of the County XI and they were supported in batting by another amateur, George Brann, and the young professional Joe Vine, and in bowling by Fred Tate, Cyril Bland and George Rubens Cox.

It was not, however, until 1899 that the results started to show. In that season Ranji succeeded Murdoch as captain and, in all first-class matches, became the first player to exceed 3,000 runs in a season. The county reached 5th place in the Championship and, of 22 Championship matches, seven were won against five lost, while Ranji scored 2,285 runs (average 76.16) and Fry 1,579 (average 42.67). Additionally, Tate and Bland each took over 90 wickets. In the following four seasons, between 1900 and 1903, Sussex reached 3rd, 4th and twice 2nd place in the Championship in what has been considered to be a 'Golden Age' of Sussex batsmanship. In 1900 Sussex won only four matches, but lost a mere two and were able to claim equal 3rd place with Kent. Ranji was now at the height of his career: Ian Peebles, writing in *The Guardian* years after-wards in 1976, took the view that Ranji could well be included in the first half-dozen greatest batsmen of all time and many have commented that his oriental style trans-formed batsmanship. Initially, instead of driving half-volleys he flicked them easily to leg and, when opposing captains began to counter this ploy by reinforcing the leg side, he drove the ball back past the bowler with uncommon power for one who, in those days at least, was lightly built. Fry was a very different kettle of fish: a classical scholar at Oxford, a sportsman and athlete of surprising versatility, the editor of his own magazine, a candidate for Parliament and, later, the commander of a naval training ship. He was also a first-class batsman of classical style. Certainly gifted, but on a less grand scale than Ranji, he batted with concentration and intelligence and was a perfect foil to the Indian maestro. It has been said that Fry's association with Ranji turned him from a good batsman into a great one.

The 1900 season saw Ranji amass 2,563 Championship runs with nine hundreds, four of them double centuries, at an average of 85.63, while Fry, less prolific, registered 1,830 runs (average 63.10), becoming the first batsman to record a double-hundred and a single hundred in the same match and scoring nine centuries altogether. Fred Tate weighed in with over 900 overs and 114 wickets at 21.71 each, while Bland accounted for 76 scalps. Although Sussex dropped one place in 1901 to 4th in the Championship they doubled their wins to eight and Ranji and Fry again ran riot with the bat, scoring respectively 2,067 runs (average 76.55) and 2,382 runs (average 74.43). Ranji recorded seven hundreds, three of them double tons, while Fry went past the hundred mark on nine occasions with two doubles and, including all first-class matches, recorded 13 centuries, six of them in succession, both achievements being records in their time. In the match with Somerset at Taunton in August Ranji made 285 not out, the highest innings for Sussex until his own nephew, Duleepsinhji, reached a triple-hundred in 1930.

A good deal has been made of Sussex reaching second place in the Championship in 1902 and 1903. In truth, they were in no way within a whisker of winning. *Wisden* clearly states the rules laid down by MCC at the time:

> One point shall be reckoned for each win, one deducted for each loss; unfinished games shall not be reckoned. The county which during the season shall have, in finished matches, obtained the greatest proportionate number of points shall be reckoned Champion county.

In 1902 Yorkshire played 25 matches, winning 13 and losing one and thus obtaining 12 points, which produced a percentage of 85.71, while Sussex won seven and lost three of 24 games played, obtaining four points and a comparatively modest percentage

Left Sussex *v.* Gloucestershire & Somerset at Hove, May 1902. From left to right, back row:
C.H.G. Bland, H.R. Butt, F.W. Marlow, R.G. Kenward, R.B. Heygate, E.H. Killick. Seated: A.E. Relf,
C.B. Fry, K.S. Ranjitsinhji (captain), F.W. Tate, J. Vine.

Right Sussex *v.* Essex at Leyton, June 1903. From left to right, back row: W. Hearne (umpire),
C.H.G. Bland, F.W. Tate, W.H. Edwards (scorer), E.H. Killick, A.E. Relf, J. Carlin (umpire). Seated:
W. Newham, H.R. Butt, K.S. Ranjitsinhji (captain), C.B. Fry, C.L.A. Smith. On ground: J. Vine,
J. Clayton (trainer), G.R. Cox.

of 40.00. However, they were significantly ahead of Nottinghamshire in 3rd place.
Nevertheless the County's achievements should not be downplayed. Ranji played in
only 11 of the 24 Championship matches, ostensibly owing to a disagreement with
some of the professionals, while Fry, apparently for reasons never wholly determined,
although both he and Ranji played in three Tests, was absent from seven matches. The
pair, however, dominated the averages, Ranji with 866 runs at 66.61 and Fry with 1,072
at 41.23, but other players certainly contributed to the success of the season. Joe Vine
with 1,083 runs at 30.08 was the leading run scorer, while George Brann, Albert Relf
and Ernest Killick all made useful runs. Fred Tate enjoyed a magnificent season with the
ball, taking 153 wickets at 14.28, his total exceeding that of Albert Relf, who was in
second place, by 97 wickets.

The following season of 1903 was, in many respects, a carbon copy of the previous
year. The Champion county, Middlesex, played a mere 16 matches, winning eight and
losing only one, thus recording a percentage of 77.77, while Sussex played 23 matches,
winning seven and losing two and reaching a percentage of 55.55, which was well
ahead of Yorkshire's percentage of 44.44 in third place. *Wisden* inclines to the view that
the County's record in 1903 was relatively not as good as that of the previous year,
despite the fact that Ranji and Fry were more often available. It was, in fact, the latter's
year, causing *Wisden* to wax lyrical about his form:

> *Everything else in Sussex cricket was dwarfed by the truly magnificent batting of C.B. Fry,*
> *even Ranjitsinhji, well as he played, being quite overshadowed. It was, of course, a big*
> *advantage for Fry to play so many of his matches at Brighton, the wickets there suffering less*

from the rain than those at most other grounds, but making full allowance for this, his record, in such a summer, of 2,413 runs in county matches, with an average of 80.43, was almost incredible.'

Fry made eight centuries, including 234 against Yorkshire at Bradford and 200 against Surrey at Hove, while recording a ninth (232 not out) for the Gentlemen *v.* Players at Lord's. What made him such an asset to Sussex was the fact that when he went past 100 he made it count, six of his nine hundreds being over 150 and three of them double-hundreds. Most people would have been happy with Ranji's return too, for he scored 1,394 runs with four hundreds at an average of 58.08. Brann, Vine and Killick were all among the runs, but the bowling relied heavily on Albert Relf with 91 wickets at 20.10 and Cox with 79 at 24.69. Fred Tate, relatively at least, had a poor year, taking 91 fewer wickets at a cost of ten more runs each than he had in 1902. Over the four seasons (1900-1903) Fry and Ranji between them made 14,587 Championship runs at an average of 69.13, scoring in the process 52 hundreds, of which 14 were double tons. It is no wonder that Sussex prospered at this time despite the fact that their bowling, often, it is true, on the batsman-friendly Hove wicket, was relatively weak. Only Fred Tate with 455 wickets in the four seasons averaged over 100 wickets per season, the next best being Albert Relf with just under 60.

From 1904 until the onset of the First World War Sussex did not make any serious challenge for the Championship, their positions ranging from a very creditable 3rd place behind Yorkshire and Lancashire in 1905 to 13th in 1907 and 1911. The reason is perhaps not difficult to find. In 1904, despite the excellent batting of both Fry and Ranji, who respectively totalled 2,376 runs (average 79.20) and 1,330 runs (average 73.88), they had continued to experience difficulty in dismissing their opponents, 15 of 24 Championship matches being drawn and only George Cox with 112 wickets and Albert Relf with 85 showing much form with the ball. From 1905 to 1907 Ranji took a sabbatical from cricket while he contested his claim to the throne of Nawanagar in India and played only in the 1908 and 1912 seasons, while Fry, after missing most of the 1906 season through injury, defected to Hampshire after 1908 so that he might be nearer his training ship *Mercury* at Hamble, near Southampton. The impact that they had made earlier was, quite evidently, greatly missed.

The guns stopped firing and the armistice was signed in November 1918, but the effect of the First World War had been considerable in Britain and cricket began again on a somewhat scaled-down schedule in the summer of 1919, only two days being allotted to Championship matches. Throughout the whole of the 1920s Sussex made no serious challenge for the Championship. In 1922 Arthur Gilligan, an incisive fast-bowler and hard-hitting lower-order batsman, became captain and, with his insistence on high-quality fielding, certainly helped Sussex to compete, but the Championship scene was dominated by Yorkshire, Lancashire and, occasionally, by Middlesex and Nottinghamshire. It was not as if Sussex did not possess some outstanding cricketers: Gilligan himself, until injured in a Gentlemen *v.* Players match at The Oval in 1924, was establishing a potent opening-bowling partnership with Maurice Tate, who had been converted in 1922 from a fairly ordinary off-spin bowler to a medium-pacer and between 1922 and 1935 took 100 wickets in the English season every year except one (and then he took 99!), while Ted Bowley, a model professional batsman and

Duleepsinhji, Ranji's nephew and arguably the best England-qualified amateur batsman between the wars, batted with great aplomb. At the same time, the two Jims, Parks and Langridge, entered the side in 1924 and were later joined by their younger brothers, Harry and John, in 1926 and 1928 respectively. If you add the ageless George Rubens Cox with his teasing slow left-arm, the steadiness of Bert Wensley's medium pace and the brilliance of Tommy Cook, it was not a bad side, but, sadly, the results did not come.

It was not, however, until 1931, the year in which Duleep inherited the captaincy, that Sussex started to challenge for honours. An entirely different system of determining the Championship from that of the 1900s was now in place. While Yorkshire romped away with the Championship with 287 points, Gloucestershire with 219, Kent with 216, Sussex with 205 and Nottinghamshire with 202 all came close together in the next four places. Sussex did not make a good start, apart from a sound victory over Lancashire at Old Trafford in the opening encounter of the season, and by the end of June, they had recorded a mere two victories. Subsequently, however, they won eight and lost only two of their remaining 16 fixtures, having the satisfaction at the beginning of July of winning four matches – against Glamorgan, Kent, Derbyshire and Essex – in succession. They recorded some hefty totals too:

477 (Bowley 137, Duleep 133) v. Essex at Hove
470 for seven declared (Duleep 162, Bowley 144) v. Surrey at The Oval
470 for seven declared (John Langridge 161, Cook 103 not out) v. Glamorgan at Cardiff
448 for six declared (Harry Parks 200 not out, Duleep 140) v. Essex at Chelmsford

Duleep led the way in the batting, but Bowley, Harry Parks and Cook all recorded 1,000-plus Championship runs, while Maurice Tate with 111 wickets, Bert Wensley with exactly 100 and Jim Langridge with 83 were the principal performers in the attack. Tate's 111 wickets cost a mere 14.75 runs each, while his economy rate of 1.68 per over was astonishingly frugal.

The next three seasons could well be called the County's second 'Golden Age.' Under three different captains they reached 2nd place in the Championship each season from 1932 to 1934. In 1932, led again by Duleep, Sussex recorded 14 wins against one loss and scored 262 points, while Yorkshire, the clear winners, won 19 matches, lost two and scored 315 points. In the end it was not a close-run affair, but whether Duleep's breakdown in health during the Somerset match at Taunton on 13-16 August, when things were at their most crucial, played any part in the final result can only be a matter of conjecture. The fact is that at the end of the Somerset game – the last match in which Duleep would ever play – Sussex, with a match in hand and 15 points potentially available were only 19 points behind Yorkshire. In the remaining five matches, in which the loss of Duleep must be considered to have been of much more than minor inconvenience, Sussex scored the full 15 points against Gloucestershire and took five points for a first-innings lead against Essex, but they conceded first-innings leads to both Warwickshire and Somerset and were well beaten – albeit without Bowley and Wensley as well as Duleep – by 167 runs against Yorkshire. Theoretically there had been 75 points to play for; in fact, Sussex gained only 26. What might have been a close contest proved finally to be nothing of the sort. Yet it was certainly not all bad. It had been a good season with Duleep, Harry Parks and Bowley all passing the 1,000-run mark,

Sussex *v.* Kent at Hastings, August 1932. From left to right: H.W. Parks, A.F. Wensley, James Langridge, W.L. Cornford, J.H. Parks, R.S.G. Scott, E.H. Bowley, T.E. Cook, K.S. Duleepsinhji (captain), M.W. Tate, A. Melville.

Sussex *v.* Northamptonshire at Hove, May 1933. From left to right, back row: T.E. Cook, H.W.Parks, James Langridge, John Langridge, J.H. Cornford, J.H. Parks, G. Cox. Seated: M.W. Tate, Sir Home Gordon, E.H. Bowley, R.S.G. Scott (captain), A.E.R. Gilligan, W.L. Cornford, A.F. Wensley.

while Maurice Tate again led the bowling with 124 wickets (average 15.58, economy rate 1.80) and the slow left-arm of the rising Jim Langridge collected 92 wickets, only a little below Tate in terms of average and economy. Fewer large totals were recorded than in 1931, but Sussex ran up 511 for seven declared (Bowley 162, Cook 160) against Warwickshire at Edgbaston, while match tallies of 13 wickets were taken by Maurice Tate (7-28 and 6-30) against Middlesex at Hove and by Jim Langridge (8-43 and 5-22) against Northamptonshire on the Wantage Road ground.

Duleep's breakdown was a tragedy for Sussex. He had endured a history of pulmonary pneumonia, something that can be easily understood when an Indian plays cricket in the relatively damp English climate and at a time when drugs were neither as plentiful nor as effective as they are nowadays. Telltale signs had occurred earlier in the summer, but Ranji had, most unwisely, encouraged his nephew to keep going. Perhaps he, too, wanted Sussex to gain their first Championship! Duleep's collapse meant that he never played cricket again; he returned sadly to India, endured an unhappy marriage and, although able to contribute to the rise of Indian cricket and serve his country on the diplomatic front, he died at the early age of fifty-four.

A new captain, Robert Scott, who had deputised for Duleep at the end of the previous season, took up the reins of leadership for 1933. Once again Yorkshire, an exceptionally fine side with batsmen such as Sutcliffe, Leyland, Barber and Mitchell, and the bowling led by the remarkable Hedley Verity, kept ahead of Sussex and recorded their third consecutive Championship, once again the struggle did not go down to the wire. Winning 18 of their first 24 Championship matches, the White Rose county romped ahead and were acclaimed Champions halfway through August. Sussex were very much the best of the rest, recording a percentage of 64.79 against the 70% by Yorkshire. A new system of scoring had been introduced in 1933: instead of all counties playing the same number of matches, as had happened from 1929 to 1932, and the side with most points being declared the Champions, they were now allowed to play differing numbers of matches and their position was determined by a percentage of their actual points score over possible points. Sussex played, in fact, 32 matches (more than any other county) against Yorkshire's 30, while two counties, Northamptonshire and Glamorgan played as few as 24! *Wisden* took the view that Sussex had hardly done themselves justice. Although they had recorded 18 wins compared to 14 in the previous season they had also lost five matches compared to one in 1932. The writer noted:

In practically all these losses, the eleven were not seen to any particular advantage. Indeed, their cricket in most of them was, not to mince matters, unworthy of a side who, as they showed in so many of their victories, could rise to heights of all-round excellence.

Despite this apparently harsh criticism by the *Wisden* correspondent, the County certainly stacked up some imposing totals:

546 (Cook 161) v. Gloucestershire at Hove
512 for three declared (Bowley 283, John Langridge 195) in the August bank holiday fixture
    v. Middlesex at Hove
481 for three declared (John Langridge 250 not out) v. Glamorgan at Hove
468 for nine declared (Cook 214, Wensley 118) v. Worcestershire at Eastbourne
457 for nine declared (Cook 143, Jim Langridge 111) v. Warwickshire at Edgbaston
445 (Jim Langridge 101) v. Nottinghamshire at Hove
441 (Jim Parks 163) v. Surrey at Hastings
421 (Jim Langridge 125) v. Lancashire at Hove

Take into account that Harry Parks scored two not-out hundreds – only the fifth batsman at the time to do so – in the Essex match at Leyton at the season's end; that Jim Langridge again took 13 wickets in a match – (6-44 and 7-64) against Somerset at Taunton; that six batsmen passed 1,000 runs (John Langridge with 1,831 and Tommy Cook with 1,795 led the way); and that two bowlers, Jim Langridge (136) and Bert Wensley (117) took 100 wickets, then it was not a bad season at all. But, of course, it wasn't a Championship victory, although Sussex beat the eventual Champions soundly on both occasions when the counties met!

Robert Scott's tenure of the captaincy was all too brief. When his father died unexpectedly he was forced to take charge of the family business, and Alan Melville, the South African, who had attended Oxford University and played for Sussex in the vacations, became the County's third captain in as many years. The 1934 season was

Sussex *v*. Yorkshire at Sheffield, June 1934. From left to right, back row: E.H. Killick (scorer), James Langridge, John Langridge, G. Cox, J.H. Cornford, H.E. Hammond (twelfth man), H.W. Parks, J.H. Parks, D.S. Richards (did not play). Seated: T.E. Cook, M.W. Tate, A. Melville (captain), A.F. Wensley, W.L. Cornford.

one in which England welcomed the Australians, who were, of course, seeking to regain the Ashes after the ill-tempered 1932/33 'Bodyline' tour in Australia. Yorkshire needed to contribute Leyland, Sutcliffe, Verity and Bowes to England's cause and, perhaps in consequence, never really challenged for the Championship. For most of the season it seemed as if Sussex might well turn their runners-up places of the previous two years into a Championship win. They held first place from 22 May, but on 14 August they ceded their lead to Lancashire who stayed at the top until the end of the season. Why did things go so badly adrift? *Wisden* commented that 'they gave the impression that they were not quite capable of producing just that extra effort necessary to carry off chief honours'. There were probably several reasons why Sussex failed to be a really tip-top side. Firstly, Ted Bowley, their great professional opening batsman who had been with the County since 1912, had effectively retired and played in just two matches, so there was a massive gap at the top of the order as John Langridge's partner and, in fact, six batsmen were tried in the opening slot. The most successful by far turned out to be Jim Parks, but he suffered a broken hand in the middle of July and five other players were at various times sidelined by injury. Secondly, Jim Langridge, 'who the previous season had been one of the outstanding all-rounders in English cricket', as noted by *Wisden*, had toured India with MCC in the previous winter, and the effort had taken a toll on his less than robust constitution, so that he performed much less well than previously, especially with the ball. Thirdly, the whole side seemed to be too aware of the position they were in and, instead of batting in their normal robust manner, developed a somewhat stodgy game, something that the new captain ought to have corrected, but perhaps he lacked the right experience to alter the situation. For all that, Cook, regarded as one of the very best players of spin bowling in the country and perhaps unlucky not to get an England cap to match the one he had gained at soccer, and John Langridge both passed 2,000 Championship runs and four others went past 1,000 runs, while Tate with 137 wickets and Jim Cornford with 81 both contributed with the ball. Away against Worcestershire in early July Sussex ran up a total of 505 (Cook 220) and exceeded 400 on a further ten occasions and were dismissed only three times for fewer than 200 runs. Their best performances were:

493 for six declared (Cook 160, Harry Parks 100 not out) v. Hampshire at Southampton

474 for seven declared (Cook 179, Wensley 103 not out) v. Warwickshire at Edgbaston

463 for five declared (Jim Parks 160, Alan Melville 105) v. Somerset at Taunton

461 for six declared v. Essex at Colchester

452 for five declared (John Langridge 160, Jim Parks 122) v. Surrey at Horsham

452 for seven declared (John Langridge 159, Jim Langridge 130) v. Kent at Maidstone

445 for five declared (John Langridge 232 not out) v. Northamptonshire at Peterborough

442 v. Gloucestershire at Cheltenham

429 for seven declared (John Langridge 148) v. Nottinghamshire at Trent Bridge

417 (Jim Langridge 149 not out) v. Worcestershire at Hastings

406 for eight declared (Jim Parks 181) v. Gloucestershire at Hove

Sussex had, in fact, missed the boat. If a side cannot convert three 2nd places into one Championship it is unlikely that they will be lucky fourth time round. Nor were they. Melville captained for one more season and then 'Jack' Holmes was in charge until the onset of the Second World War. A 5th place in 1937, when Jim Parks recorded his unbeatable double of 3,000 runs and 100 wickets in a season, was their best effort.

After six blank seasons during the war much had changed. 'Billy' Griffith, a war hero and splendid 'keeper, was in charge, but the captaincy and the secretaryship were too much for any one man. Sussex finished last in 1946 and Griffith resigned. They did very little better, in fact, until 1953, being in 9th place or below for six seasons. This period, too, contained one of Sussex's civil wars when the committee were ousted and Hugh Bartlett lost the captaincy at the 1950 AGM. Fortunately for Sussex, Jim Langridge was on hand and was appointed their first full-time professional captain – a post that he held with distinction for three seasons.

Then, in 1953, came the David Sheppard year and Sussex again reached out for high honours. Sheppard was remarkable: not long down from Cambridge, where he had led the side with distinction, destined for the Church and at the age of twenty-four younger than most of his side, he possessed in full the powers of leadership both on and off the field. Surrey, the eventual Champions, were challenged throughout the season by Sussex, but the drawn game between the counties at Hove meant that the County were never going to muster quite enough points to head off their rivals. In the end 16 points separated them and this was at a time when a win counted 12 and a first-innings lead four. It was a good season, however, judged by most standards. Richard Langridge, Jim's son, argues cogently that the revival in the County's fortunes began in the August and September during his father's captaincy in 1952. Although Sussex finished 13th in the Championship in that season, they played particularly well from the end of July onwards, beating Kent, Hampshire and Middlesex in succession, having the best of some rain-affected draws with Lancashire and Yorkshire, saving the match well against Worcestershire, succumbing to the rain against Essex and then beating Glamorgan, Lancashire and Derbyshire for three more victories in succession. It certainly got them in a winning frame of mind. Sussex's success in 1953 was founded on the outstanding batting of Sheppard, who was well supported by Ken Suttle, John Langridge and the junior Jim Parks and George Cox, the sons of famous fathers. The bowling was headed by Ian Thomson, Ted James and Jim Wood, while the two off-spinners Alan Oakman and Robin Marlar also weighed in with over 50 wickets each. Although large totals, such as those obtained in the 1930s, were rather fewer and further between, the County totalled:

404 for seven declared (Parks 97) *v.* Essex at Ilford
402 for six declared (Jim Langridge 104 not out, Suttle 103) *v.* Somerset at Taunton
393 for eight declared (John Langridge 127) *v.* Derbyshire at Derby
387 for three declared (Sheppard 181 not out, Cox 144) *v.* Yorkshire at Hastings

Perhaps the most exciting innings total, however, was against Leicestershire at Leicester when Sussex, having been 109 runs in arrears on first innings, responded to Charles Palmer's declaration and reached 346 for two (Sheppard 186 not out) to win in just under four hours by eight wickets. The 1953 season was, however, another case of 'so near and yet so far', and sadly Sussex did not seriously challenge for honours for another twenty-eight years.

In this long intervening period there were a few highlights. Robin Marlar led the County to 4th place in 1955 and Ted Dexter achieved the same placing on two occasions – in 1960 and 1963 – but for the rest it makes rather bleak reading with Sussex often well into the lower half of the Championship, until in 1979 and 1980, after a largely unsatisfactory period under Tony Greig's captaincy, Sussex again reached 4th place under Arnold Long. Greig was glamorous and an excellent all-rounder, but he saved many of his best performances for England, often playing in little more than half the County's matches. Interestingly, his batting average for England was in excess of 40, for Sussex a modest 28. When Long, a cast-off wicketkeeper from Surrey, assumed the captaincy, however, his canny and thoughtful leadership started to lead Sussex back to near the top.

Arnold Long had built a platform and Sussex's new captain in 1981, John Barclay, intelligent, enthusiastic and a more than useful all-rounder, was keen to profit from the work of his predecessor. Unlike the previous occasions when Sussex had achieved 2nd place, this season was a neck-and-neck struggle throughout with Nottinghamshire, who were led by the capable South African Clive Rice. The end result could have gone either way; finally the Midlanders triumphed by two points.

The facts are these: each side had a programme of 22 matches and each won 11 matches. Nottinghamshire lost four and drew six and had one match abandoned; Sussex, however, lost only three, drew six and, crucially as things panned out, had two matches abandoned. Matches where no play at all was possible in the 1981 scheme of things provided no points to either side, whereas nowadays each side would score four points. The fact that Sussex had one more match abandoned than Nottinghamshire would in itself, had the present system obtained, have secured the Championship for Sussex. But this was sadly not the case. Following the progress of the two counties during the season (they were certainly not at the top throughout) it can be noted that, by the end of May, Nottinghamshire had played four matches (one abandoned) and scored 31 points, while Sussex's four matches (two abandoned) had produced 24 points – round one to Nottinghamshire. By the end of June each side had played five further matches and Nottinghamshire were on 81 points, Sussex on 88 – round two to Sussex. The end of July saw Nottinghamshire play six matches to Sussex's five and lead by 164 to 153 (round three to Nottinghamshire), while each side played six matches in August,

Sussex v. Lancashire, Liverpool, May 1953. From left to right, back row: A.E. James, J.M. Parks, A.S.M. Oakman, N.I. Thomson, K.G. Suttle, R.T. Webb. Seated: G. Cox, James Langridge, D.S. Sheppard (captain), John Langridge, D.J. Wood.

Sussex 1981 at Hove. From left to right, back row: S.J. Storey (coach), C.M. Wells, T.D. Booth-Jones, G.C. Arnold, G. le Roux, Imran Khan, C.P. Phillipson. Front row: I.J. Gould, I.A. Greig, J.R.T. Barclay (captain), P.W.G. Parker, C.E. Waller, G.D. Mendis.

and at the month's end the Midlanders had moved to 283 points against Sussex's 255, but the southern county had a match in hand. Sussex potentially had 48 points to gain and scored 47, Nottinghamshire 24 and scored 21. Final result: Nottinghamshire 304 to Sussex's 302. Batting points were led by Sussex (58 to 56), bowling by Nottinghamshire (72 to 68). It had been a close-run thing.

Were Sussex unlucky not to win on this occasion? An impartial voice might say that Sussex, with the loss of two abandoned matches, where they would most probably have scraped three vital points had the matches been played, had not enjoyed the rub of the green. Over and above all this, as Sussex's John Barclay has shown so cleverly in his recent book *The Appeal of the Championship,* there was the encounter between the two protagonists at Trent Bridge in August. Rice won the toss for Notts and invited the visitors to bat and, although Gehan Mendis scored an excellent 65, Sussex were dismissed for 208. Sussex came back strongly as Chris Waller and Barclay exploited the turn in the pitch, and only Basharat Hassan with 58 not out showed any resistance, Notts succumbing to 108 all out. Six bonus points to Sussex and four to Notts. Sussex did not prosper in their second innings and, although Ian Greig with 43 and Ian Gould with 42 batted soundly, they were all out for 144. This, however, left the hosts to score 251 – the highest total of the match – to win on the final day. Imran Khan removed Paul Todd and Derek Randall with successive deliveries, Notts were six for two wickets and Sussex seemed in control. A 3rd-wicket stand, however, between Hassan and Tim Robinson added 67 and the former then added a further 101 with Rice. Notts were making good progress and, despite poor light, refused offers to leave the field. When Imran bowled Hassan for 79 and the Notts innings subsided from 174 for four to 205 for seven they decided to go off. Seven of the final 20 overs were lost and, although nine wickets were down for 210, Eddie Hemmings and Mike Bore survived the final four overs. Notts had scrambled a draw. Barclay describes the final appeal of the match:

> Imran ran in. Legs pumping and arms rolling, a touch of Michael Holding in his style, he accelerated towards the crease and released the ball at terrifying speed. Bore plainly never saw it, but instinctively he went back towards his stumps. The ball hit him beneath the knee roll of his back leg with a resounding thud. The whole of the Sussex team to a man filled their lungs and let out an appeal to shake the leaves off the trees. All the energy and excitement, the triumphs and the upsets, the sheer euphoria of that thrilling summer found voice in one appeal. Sussex Champions? We were filled with hope. The crowd drew in a breath, and all eyes turned upon the hapless umpire, Peter Stevens.

It was the appeal of the season all right, but Sussex have had to wait for another twenty-two years. Between 1982 and 2001 Sussex enjoyed no great success. Under John Barclay's leadership (1982-1986) they ranged from 6th to 11th place, but there then followed five disastrous seasons in which the County recorded two bottom places and one next to bottom. The advent of Alan Wells as skipper in 1992 saw a modest improvement, but poor performances in 1995 and 1996 led to a stormy AGM in early 1997 when Wells lost the captaincy and, rather like a rerun of 1950, the committee were again put out to grass. Peter Moores, the new captain, valiantly tried to rally a side bereft of many of its top players, but in vain. Sussex were again at the bottom, although one county director of cricket expressed the view that Moores deserved a season's award for his brave efforts. For 1998 he gave way as skipper to Chris Adams, brought in by Tony Pigott from Derbyshire, and for two seasons some modest success was achieved. With the arrival of the two-tier Championship in 2000 Sussex were plumb bottom of Division Two, but true to their inconsistent ways, they turned things round a season later and won the Division Two Championship and with it promotion to Division One. Some rather overzealous Sussex supporters claimed a Championship win, but wiser heads knew that the battle was only half won.

In 2002 Surrey romped away with the Championship and Sussex, who had endured the tragic loss of Umer Rashid in a pre-season accident, ended the season in 6th place in Division One, that is to say, just above the three relegated counties, Hampshire, Somerset and Yorkshire. But for two factors they themselves might have been close to going down. The first occurred during Hampshire's match with Lancashire at the Rose Bowl, their new ground in Southampton. Forty wickets fell for 629 runs and the ECB docked the home side eight points for a 'poor' pitch. They were perhaps a trifle unfortunate as Lancashire won the match comfortably. This deduction in itself, had it not occurred, would not have brought about Sussex's relegation, but the second factor was their win, rather against the odds, against Surrey, the eventual Champions. If both factors had not worked in Sussex's favour they could well have been relegated in place of Hampshire.

In the event, the Sussex-Surrey encounter saw 17 wickets crash on the first day as James Kirtley and Kevin Innes bowled Surrey out for 193 and Sussex replied with 139 for seven wickets. On the second morning some resilient batting by Innes and Mark Davis lifted the County to a ten-run lead. When the visitors batted for a second time they showed much greater application and, aided by half-centuries from Ian Ward and Mark Ramprakash, reached 261 for eight by the close. It was beginning to look like another strong Surrey recovery. On the third morning Mushtaq Ahmed, the former Pakistan leg-spinner, who was standing in for his colleague Saqlain Mushtaq and had been 17 not out overnight, contributed a well-made 47 and the visitors' innings ended on 296. Sussex, needing 287, not the highest total of the match, but still a tall order, lost Richard Montgomerie and Tony Cottey before the close of the third day, leaving them on 85 for two wickets, with Murray Goodwin unbeaten on 42. On a tense final morning Sussex crawled from 85 to 145 for three, crucially losing only one wicket, that of Matthew Prior, in the first session. After lunch Goodwin was joined by Chris Adams, the Sussex skipper. The pair counter-attacked and, although Goodwin was dismissed immediately on reaching his century and Adams fell on 62, momentum had been achieved and the middle order saw Sussex home by four wickets. Interestingly, *Wisden* commented that 'Tudor and Mushtaq produced spells of Test quality'. In the match Tudor took seven wickets but Mushtaq, in the course of 42 overs, conceded 119 and failed to take a wicket. In fact, in his two matches for Surrey, he took eight wickets for 305 runs (average 38.12). It was therefore with some surprise that Sussex members heard that he had been engaged by the County as the second overseas player in 2003 to augment the batsmanship of Murray Goodwin. Players from the subcontinent are said – evidently, however, not always correctly – to mature and then to fade rather earlier than their English counterparts. A good many sensed that Mushtaq, whose thirty-third birthday would occur in June 2003, despite an admirable career both with Pakistan and Somerset, might now be just a little 'over the hill.' Furthermore, it was thought that the Sussex batting, which had, it is true, exceeded 600 runs in an innings in two matches in 2002, but had also been dismissed for fewer than 200 runs on four occasions and for fewer than 300 in 11 matches, might not be able to supply the back-up to an essentially profligate leg-spinner who might well haemorrhage runs at certain times. How totally wrong the doom merchants were shown to be! Mushtaq, aided by the prospect of some hefty bonuses, bamboozled county batsmen of every sort, became the first bowler to take 100 wickets in the County Championship since Andrew Caddick of Somerset had achieved the feat in 1998 and scored a hatful of runs into the bargain. This, together with Sussex's exuberant batting, especially from Murray Goodwin and the middle order, where Matthew Prior had a wonderful season, saw the County gradually gain pace after a slow start and, winning four of their last five matches, leave Lancashire and Surrey, their immediate challengers, floundering in their wake. An individual milestone was also reached when Goodwin, in the innings against Leicestershire which assured Sussex of victory, amassed 335 not out and went past Duleepsinhji's 333 which had been made seventy-three years previously. It was a truly memorable and marvellous year.

SUSSEX v. MIDDLESEX AT LORD'S

Wednesday to Saturday, 23 to 26 April 2003

Sussex began the 2003 season with what director of cricket Peter Moores described as the strongest squad they had possessed for several seasons. Their first match took them to the 'Cathedral of Cricket' against a Middlesex side who had gained promotion from Division Two in 2002.

It was St George's Day and Chris Adams, on winning the toss for Sussex, decided to bat. It was not, however, a wholly British occasion. On view were thirteen players who had been born abroad and it was perhaps fitting that it was James Kirtley and Jason Lewry, from Eastbourne and Worthing respectively, who were, albeit later on, the heroes of the day. A sunlit early summer's day was surely a time for good cricket, but Richard Montgomerie and Murray Goodwin made hard work of the Middlesex opening attack of Joe Dawes, a thirty-two-year-old Queenslander, and Chad Keegan, a native of Johannesburg. After Zimbabwe-born Goodwin was surprised by a lifter from Dawes, Montgomerie chased an out-swinger and Cottey perished first ball, Sussex had reached 53 for three after 22 overs. The home side's second string caused fewer problems and skipper Adams and Tim Ambrose, from Eastbourne via New South Wales, enjoyed some loose offerings from Cook and Abdul Razzaq of Pakistan, but an athletic caught-and-bowled by Weekes saw off the Sussex skipper and, although Ambrose reached a well-crafted half-century, Robin Martin-Jenkins pulled a long-hop to mid-wicket and the rest of the Sussex batting tried – relatively unsuccessfully – to hit their way out of trouble. It was then left to Kirtley, who played straight, and Lewry, who hit hard, to lift a poor 172 for nine into a modest 239. When Lewry heaved into the outfield he was just two short of his career best, but a total of 239 and only one batting point was hardly what Sussex had hoped to begin the season with.

The batting heroes were soon at work when Middlesex went in and skipper Strauss and former England one-day hopeful Owais Shah were soon back in the hutch. At 69 for two Middlesex seemed to be making a reasonable recovery, but the late loss of Nash and nightwatchman Cook left them at the close on 79 for four, only South African Koenig with his ECB Italian passport showing determined resistance. On the Thursday morning the hosts soon subsided to 116 all out and Sussex, who were doubtless pleased to have collected three bowling points with some ease, were soon at the crease again. The bristling Middlesex opening attack soon had them in trouble on what was proving to be a helpful seamers' wicket, as Middlesex had found to their cost, and, although Cottey and Ambrose batted soundly for modest 30s it was left to Martin-Jenkins to take toll of the less accurate Razzaq and Cook. For all his efforts, however, Sussex could do no better than 194 for nine off 59 overs by the close.

Dismissed on the Friday morning for 204 and therefore with an overall lead of 327 the smart money had to be on Sussex, but after the cheap dismissal of Koenig an excellent 2nd-wicket partnership between Strauss and Shah added 117 before Kevin Innes trapped the latter for 61 in mid-afternoon, at which point rain brought a conclusion to

Opposite Kevin Innes appeals successfully for lbw against Owais Shah in Sussex's first match of the season against Middlesex at Lord's in April.

the day's play. A subtle change in the weather had eased batting conditions so that the ball, both through the air and off the pitch, did far less than it had on the Thursday. The result was that the highest total of the match, rarely achieved in a fourth innings, was now a distinct possibility. Although Sussex stuck to their task their fielding showed some imperfections and failures of line and length were punished gratefully by the Middlesex pair. It was clear that the first session of play on Saturday would be of vital importance to both sides.

Kirtley, who might have felt at this early part of the season that the success of Lancashire's Jimmy Anderson during the winter tour had now ended his international prospects – happily this proved not to be the case – bowled with determination all day. He quickly won an lbw decision against Strauss, not out overnight, and while Middlesex seemed for the most part to be ahead of the game, they never dominated, scoring only 38 runs in the first hour, 39 in the second, 30 in the third and 46 in the fourth. By this time Kirtley had won three more lbw decisions against Joyce (three hours for 49), Razzaq and Weekes and, at 288 for seven, Middlesex were still not quite out of the woods, but Cook, who hit three fours off the tiring Kirtley, and Hutton saw them home with an 8th-wicket partnership of 42. Mushtaq, who had bowled tidily in Middlesex's first innings and had bamboozled Nash early on, appeared relatively tame after that and conceded 97 runs from just over 28 overs, although a septic nail on his spinning finger made bowling a painful experience for him. One correspondent, sadly without the aid of foresight, was bold enough to write that Mushtaq in his former pomp would never have let his opponents off the hook. What later occurred is, of course, another story.

The fact of the matter is that Sussex, despite the change in weather conditions which doubtless favoured Middlesex more than a little, should never have lost this match. Despite his side's failure Chris Adams, in speaking to *The Kent and Sussex Courier,* was relatively upbeat. 'The most disappointing aspect,' he said, 'was not winning after being in a seemingly good position. The ball was cutting both ways a lot for the first two-and-a-half days, and then, inexplicably, the pitch flattened out. On the last day we still went past the edge dozens of times and on other days we would have won.'

Middlesex (17 points) beat Sussex (4 points) by three wickets.

40p   Frizzell County Championship   **40p**
MIDDLESEX v. SUSSEX
Wednesday, Thursday, Friday & Saturday, April 23, 24, 25 & 26, 2003   (4-day Match)

SUSSEX

	First Innings		Second Innings	
1 R. R. Montgomerie (7)	c Nash b Keegan	20	b Keegan	2
2 M. W. Goodwin (3)	c Shah b Dawes	16	lbw b Dawes	23
3 P. A. Cottey (2)	lbw b Dawes	0	b Cook	38
†4 C. J. Adams (1)	c and b Weekes	26	lbw b Razzaq	12
5 T. R. Ambrose (11)	b Cook	51	lbw b Dawes	35
6 R. S. C. Martin-Jenkins (12)	c Hutton b Dawes	13	lbw b Weekes	50
*7 M. J. Prior (13)	c Razzaq b Weekes	11	lbw b Keegan	4
8 K. J. Innes (15)	st Nash b Weekes	15	c Hutton b Keegan	1
9 Mushtaq Ahmed (9)	c Nash b Keegan	9	c Nash b Keegan	2
10 R. J. Kirtley (6)	not out	20	not out	25
11 J. D. Lewry (5)	c Hutton b Razzaq	45	c Nash b Dawes	8
Bonus Points 4	B , l-b 11, w , n-b 2,	13	B , l-b 4, w , n-b ,	4
	Total ....(73.1 overs)	**239**	Total ....(62.1 overs)	**204**

FALL OF THE WICKETS
1—37   2—41   3—41   4—92   5—132   6—138   7—154   8—168   9—172   10—239
1—24   2—28   3—63   4—79   5—123   6—132   7—136   8—146   9—186   10—204

ANALYSIS OF BOWLING	1st Innings					2nd Innings				
Name	O.	M.	R.	W.	Wd. N-b	O.	M.	R.	W.	Wd. N-b
Dawes	22	4	58	3	... ...	15.1	3	47	3	... ...
Keegan	19	4	49	2	... ...	21	8	36	4	... ...
Cook	13	2	42	1	... ...	10	0	45	1	... ...
Razzaq	9.1	0	43	1	... 1	11	0	55	1	... ...
Weekes	10	1	36	3	... ...	3	1	7	1	... ...
Hutton	...	...	...	...	... ...	2	0	10	0	

MIDDLESEX

	First Innings		Second Innings	
†1 A. J. Strauss	c Prior b Kirtley	10	lbw b Kirtley	83
2 S. G. Koenig	lbw b Kirtley	43	c Prior b Lewry	7
3 O. A. Shah	b Lewry	1	lbw b Innes	61
*4 D. C. Nash	b M-Jenkins	17	b Mushtaq	29
5 S. J. Cook	b Mushtaq	5	not out	22
6 E. C. Joyce	lbw b Kirtley	8	lbw b Kirtley	49
7 Abdul Razzaq	lbw b Lewry	3	lbw b Kirtley	11
8 P. N. Weekes	run out	0	lbw b Kirtley	33
9 B. L. Hutton	lbw b Mushtaq	2	not out	11
10 C. B. Keegan	c Prior b Mushtaq	8		
11 J. H. Dawes	not out	3		
Bonus Points 3	B 1, l-b 4, w 1, n-b 10,	16	B 8, l-b 11, w 1, n-b 4,	24
	Total ....(48.3 overs)	**116**	Total .(7 wkts, 106.4 overs)	**330**

FALL OF THE WICKETS
1—24   2—29   3—69   4—74   5—92   6—97   7—97   8—98   9—109   10—116
1—19   2—136   3—165   4—200   5—225   6—287   7—288   8—   9—   10—

ANALYSIS OF BOWLING	1st Innings					2nd Innings				
Name	O.	M.	R.	W.	Wd. N-b	O.	M.	R.	W.	Wd. N-b
Lewry	17	8	34	2	... 1	25	4	50	1	1 ...
Kirtley	16	3	51	3	1 4	33	10	87	4	... 1
Mushtaq	10.3	4	16	3	... ...	28.4	6	97	1	... 1
Martin-Jenkins	5	2	10	1	... ...	10	2	42	0	... ...
Innes	...	...	...	...	... ...	10	2	35	1	... ...
	...	...	...	...	... ...	...	...	...	...	... ...

Umpires—B. Dudleston & V. A. Holder   Scorers—M. J. Smith & J. F. Hartridge
†Captain   *Wicket-keeper
Play begins at 11.00 each day. Luncheon Interval 1st, 2nd & 3rd days 1.15—1.55, 4th day 1.00—1.40
Tea Interval 1st, 2nd & 3rd days 4.10—4.30, or when 32 overs remain to be bowled,
whichever is the later. 4th day 3.40—4.00.
Stumps drawn 1st, 2nd & 3rd days at 6.30, or after 104 overs have been bowled;
4th day at 6.00 or after 96 overs have been bowled. The captains may agree to end the
match at 5.30 on the 4th day if there is no prospect of a result.
If play is suspended for any reason the minimum number of overs to be bowled in the
day shall be reduced by one over for each 3¾ minutes of play lost.

Sussex won the toss

Middlesex won by 3 wickets

SUSSEX *v.* KENT AT HOVE

Wednesday to Friday, 30 April to 2 May 2003

On the back of an annoying defeat by Middlesex at Lord's in a match which Sussex might well have – and perhaps ought to have – won, they came back to headquarters at Hove to take on Kent. Skipper Chris Adams had previously said that Kent were likely to be a tougher nut to crack than recently promoted Middlesex, but cricket does not always follow the obvious path.

Mark Ealham, captaining Kent in the absence of David Fulton, who had suffered retinal damage when a ball from a bowling machine had found its way past his facial guard, won the toss and decided to give Sussex first innings on what proved to be a slow pitch. Ealham opened with Martin Saggers and Ben Trott and the former soon dismissed Murray Goodwin. When Trott proved expensive and nine overs had been bowled the ball was thrown to Alamgir Sheriyar, the left-arm pace bowler signed by Kent from Worcestershire in the close season, and with his fifth delivery he bowled Richard Montgomerie, who offered no stroke. Having been given the Sea End with the wind behind him, Sheriyar made the ball kick disconcertingly and with the total on 83 he accounted for Tony Cottey. In the meantime Chris Adams, who had survived a run out first ball when Cottey sent him back, batted with accustomed gusto, but enjoyed a stroke of luck on 42 when a ball from Ealham nudged the stumps but failed to dislodge a bail. Adams smashed the first ball after lunch for four to reach a 79-ball fifty, but was – not for the first time – caught at slip in the next over. The middle part of the innings was cemented by Tim Ambrose and Matthew Prior who both contributed forties, although in the latter's case some good fortune was involved as he clipped his third ball to Carberry at square leg who failed to hang on to the catch. Prior and Mushtaq, who hit seven fours – four in an over off James Tredwell – in his 37 in 39 balls, added a useful 49 for the 8th wicket so that Sussex finally claimed two batting points and reached a satisfactory but not obviously match-winning 279. Sheriyar claimed his first five-wicket haul for his new county and might have had seven if Kent's fielding had been better.

Kent's innings was opened by Michael Carberry, signed from Surrey, and Robert Key, who had enjoyed a modest but not wholly unprofitable winter with England in Australia and was clearly looking to advance his Test claims. Unfortunately he shouldered arms to James Kirtley and saw his off stump disappear, while Carberry gloved a lifting ball from Jason Lewry down the leg side to the 'keeper. When Adams, among the best second slips in the country, picked up Ed Smith off Kevin Innes for a cameo 23, Kent had subsided to 29 for three, but solid batting by Australian Greg Blewett and Matthew Walker steadied the ship and at 81 for three at the close there seemed to be all to play for on the Thursday morning.

Resuming on a bright and breezy day Kent might have prospered rather more than they did. Blewett sparred meekly at Kirtley and Ealham pushed forward with pad and not bat, while Geraint Jones played all round an in-swinger. Walker who had batted solidly for his 40 was out in almost farcical manner. Having edged to slip and taken a single from which four overthrows resulted he was asked by umpire John Hampshire to face again and, two balls later, was promptly caught by Montgomerie. The rest of the Kent innings petered out tamely, apart from Tredwell's neat innings in which he struck

James Kirtley appeals hard against Kent.

Mushtaq out of the ground. Sussex led on first innings by 94 runs and had collected five bonus points.

Mindful perhaps that a 123-run first-innings lead against Middlesex had resulted in defeat, Sussex set out purposefully on their second innings, and at 166 for four wickets they seemed to be succeeding. At this point they started to flounder. Robin Martin-Jenkins under-edged a pull into his stumps and Matt Prior was stumped – precisely as Adams had been earlier – overbalancing as he played forward to Tredwell. Innes and Mushtaq were quickly dismissed and, when Goodwin, who had batted securely on a seaming pitch, heaved across the line four short of his hundred and was lbw to Tredwell in the final over, a promising position had been completely squandered.

Above Robin Martin-Jenkins batting against Kent at Hove in Sussex's first win of the season at the end of April and the beginning of May.

Below Sussex fielders crowd a Kent batsman at Hove.

Mushtaq comes in to bowl past umpire John Hampshire against Kent at Hove.

On the Friday morning Kirtley and Lewry added 24 for the last wicket so that Kent were set 293 to win, the highest total of the match. The Hove pitch was sluggish, but never really spiteful or wholly difficult. It was, however, no easy task for Kent and no batsman appeared able to play the sort of grafting innings that Goodwin had played on the previous day when he had held the Sussex innings together. Key played classily for his 28 and, when Blewett and Smith were together, a substantial partnership appeared as if it might develop but in fact it added only 62 in 20 overs. Mushtaq snared the Australian with a bat-pad catch, Walker played on and Smith and Jones departed in a dramatic Kirtley over which featured two wickets, a wide, a missed catch, another spectacular one and, finally, left two Sussex fielders injured. Cottey damaged his thumb as he tried to hang on to a catch at square leg off Smith, who two balls later spooned Kirtley to extra cover, while Jones, after a further two balls, attempted to hook Kirtley and Lewry, sprinting round from mid-on, brought off a spectacular diving catch. Unfortunately, he was struck in the face by the knee of the substitute fielder Carl Hopkinson who, from the mid-wicket position, thought it was his catch. The pace of Kirtley and the guile of Mushtaq had proved too much for Kent, and Sussex ran out winners by 133 runs before the close of the third day.

Sussex, having firmly put the Middlesex defeat behind them, played the more disciplined cricket and were worthy winners and the recipients of 19 points. Sussex's vice-captain, James Kirtley, who took nine wickets in the match and moved into the

Tim Ambrose pulls to the boundary against Kent at Hove.

SUSSEX v KENT

at Hove on 30th April - 3rd May - Frizzell County Championship Division 1

Kent won the toss and elected to bowl

* Captain, + Wicket-Keeper   [Sussex's squad numbers listed in square brackets]

SUSSEX

#	Player	1st Innings	Runs	2nd Innings	Runs
1	R.R. Montgomerie [7]	b: Sheriyar	22	b: Sheriyar	12
2	M.W. Goodwin [3]	b: Saggers	9	Lbw b: Tredwell	96
3	P.A. Cottey [2]	c: Ealham b: Sheriyar	19	Lbw b: Sheriyar	2
4	C.J. Adams * [1]	c: Blewett b: Sheriyar	54	st: Jones b: Tredwell	11
5	T.R. Ambrose [11]	c: Jones b: Saggers	41	c: Blewett b: Saggers	5
6	R.S.C. Martin-Jenkins [12]	c: Jones b: Sheriyar	16	b: Ealham	34
7	M.J. Prior + [13]	c: Jones b: Ealham	40	st: Jones b: Tredwell	4
8	K.J. Innes [15]	c: Walker b: Ealham	9	Lbw b: Ealham	1
9	Mushtaq Ahmed [9]	c: Jones b: Saggers	37	c: Blewett b: Ealham	0
10	R.J. Kirtley [6]	not out	7	not out	14
11	J.D. Lewry [5]	b: Sheriyar	22	c: Jones b: Tredwell	10
12	M.J.G. Davis [8]				

	b 1	lb 0	wd 0	nb 2	Extras	3	b 0	lb 4	wd 0	nb 0	Extras	4
	Overs	72.2		Provisional Total		279	Overs	64.1		Provisional Total		198
	Pens	0	Wkts	10	Total	279	Pens	0	Wkts	10	Total	198

Fall of wickets 1st Inns: 1 - 25 2 - 42 3 - 83 4 -134 5 -158 6 -166 7 -193 8 -242 9 -256 10-279

2nd Inns: 1 - 28 2 - 35 3 - 55 4 - 84 5 -166 6 -171 7 -174 8 -174 9 -174 10-198

Bonus Points - Sussex 2, Kent 3

Bowling	Ovs	Md	R	Wk	wd	nb	Ovs	Md	R	Wk	wd	nb
Saggers	20	3	77	3	0	1	13	4	49	1	0	0
Trott	9	0	53	0	0	0	8	2	29	0	0	0
Sheriyar	20.2	5	65	5	0	0	14	3	34	2	0	0
Ealham	14	4	45	2	0	0	10	3	34	3	0	0
Tredwell	9	2	38	0	0	0	19.1	4	48	4	0	0

KENT

1st Innings   2nd Innings   Target 293

#	Player	1st Innings	Runs	2nd Innings	Runs
1	M.A. Carberry	c: Prior b: Lewry	3	c: Prior b: Kirtley	3
2	R.W.T. Key	b: Kirtley	0	b: Lewry	28
3	E.T. Smith	c: Adams b: Innes	23	c: Ambrose b: Kirtley	33
4	G.S. Blewett	c: Prior b: Kirtley	41	c: Montgomerie b: Mushtaq	37
5	M.J. Walker	c: Adams b: Kirtley	40	b: Walker	11
6	M.A. Ealham *	Lbw b: Mushtaq	24	Lbw b: Mushtaq	15
7	G.O. Jones +	b: Lewry	2	c: Lewry b: Kirtley	0
8	J.C. Tredwell	not out	32	Lbw b: Kirtley	10
9	B.J. Trott	(10) b: Innes	0	(10) b: Kirtley	0
10	M.J. Saggers	(9) Lbw b: Mushtaq	9	(9) c: Prior b: Kirtley	1
11	A. Sheriyar	Lbw b: Mushtaq	2	not out	7
12	A. Khan				

	b 0	lb 7	wd 0	nb 2	Extras	9	b 9	lb 4	wd 1	nb 0	Extras	14
	Overs	67.5		Provisional Total		185	Overs	49.5		Provisional Total		159
	Pens	0	Wkts	10	Total	185	Pens	0	Wkts	10	Total	159

Fall of wickets 1st Inns: 1 - 2 2 - 10 3 -29 4 -105 5 -114 6 -119 7 -163 8 -181 9 -182 10-185

2nd Inns: 1 -31 2 -35 3 -97 4 - 111 5 -123 6 -124 7 -145 8 -147 9 -147 10-159

Bonus Points - Sussex 3

Bowling	Ovs	Md	R	Wk	wd	nb	Ovs	Md	R	Wk	wd	nb
Lewry	13	2	44	2	0	0	14	1	59	1	0	0
Kirtley	17	6	41	3	0	1	15	4	26	6	1	0
Innes	7	1	18	2	0	0	3	0	14	0	0	0
Martin-Jenkins	12	2	31	0	0	0	4	2	5	0	0	0
Mushtaq	18.5	3	44	3	0	0	13.5	2	42	3	0	0

SUSSEX WON BY 133 RUNS

UMPIRES :
J.H. Hampshire
P.J. Hartley
SCORERS :
J.F. Hartridge
J. Foley

HOURS OF PLAY
Days 1 - 3: 11am - 6.30pm
Day 4 : 11am - 6pm
Lunch
Days 1 - 3: 1.15pm - 1.55pm
Day 4 : 1pm - 1.40pm
Tea
Days 1 - 3 : 4.10pm - 4.30pm
or when 32 overs remain to be bowled, whichever is later
Day 4: 3.40pm - 4pm

1st Inns Bonus Pts
(Only in the first 130 Overs)
Batting (Max 5pts)
1pt at achieving 200, 250, 300, 350 and 400 runs.
Bowling (Max 3pts)
1 pt for taking 3, 6 & 9 wkts

position of the leading wicket-taker in Division One, was well satisfied and told the media: 'This is a massive win for us – especially as, last night, the game was looking eerily like the one at Lord's. Goodwin's innings was the best of the match and Mushtaq has made a big difference already.'

Sussex (19 points) beat Kent (3 points) by 133 runs.

SUSSEX v. WARWICKSHIRE AT EDGBASTON

Friday to Monday, 9 to 12 May 2003

Sussex went from brilliance against Kent at Hove to banality in their clash with Warwickshire a mere seven days later. Winning the toss, Ashley Giles, the England slow left-armer, captaining the Midland county in the absence of regular skipper Michael Powell, had no hesitation in taking first use of the Edgbaston pitch. Although James Kirtley dismissed Tony Frost when he had put on 86 for the 1st wicket with Jonathan Trott, that was the only success for the visitors before lunch. Trott, formerly an South African Under-19 batsman, now with an EU passport and able to qualify for England, is said to be a distant relative of the Australian cricketers Albert and Harry Trott – an engaging mixture of nationalities which seem nowadays to abound in the county game. He proceeded boldly towards his maiden first-class hundred, reaching 97 at lunch and achieving it soon afterwards. His 2nd-wicket stand with Mark Wagh had been worth 108 runs. What was more, he became the first Warwickshire player since Brian Lara nine years previously to score a hundred on Championship debut.

If the morning certainly belonged to the hosts, Trott being particularly severe on Robin Martin-Jenkins, whom he pulled for three fours and a six, after lunch Mushtaq set about unpicking the Warwickshire innings, dismissing Trott, Wagh, Bell, Ostler and Brown by taking five wickets for 27 in the course of 60 balls. Troughton and the late order, however, all batted sensibly, but Sussex, having claimed their full bowling points, must have been relieved that their opponents had reached no more than 350 for nine wickets at the close.

The Saturday morning, however, saw Sussex do nothing to stop the home side from seizing the initiative. Mushtaq had bowled Sussex back into the match on the previous day, but he soon dropped a return catch from Mo Sheikh, 39 not out overnight, who then batted so well with Alan Richardson that 74 were added for the last wicket in 16 overs. Warwickshire, at one stage on 269 for seven, finally reached an impressive 422. When Sussex's turn came, they batted carefully to reach 116 for three wickets at the close and still 306 behind, Chris Adams being bowled by the last ball of a day which had been shorn of the last 35 overs.

Tony Cottey and nightwatchman Kirtley batted soundly enough on the Sunday morning to ensure that Sussex went past the 200 mark, but at 235 for six they were still in danger of following on, until a 7th-wicket stand of 125 between the two young wicketkeeper-batsmen, Tim Ambrose and Matt Prior, brought them to their first 300 of the season and past 350 and four batting points. Ambrose, who had given Prior a 21-over start, batted watchfully, while Prior took the attack to the Warwickshire bowlers and overtook his partner in the eighties. Both deserved hundreds perhaps, but Ambrose was lbw and Prior caught after striking two sixes and 14 fours, as the last four wickets fell for seven runs. The hosts progressed to 79 for three wickets at the close and the match seemed to be drifting towards a draw.

Warwickshire's young England hopefuls, Ian Bell and Jim Troughton, had eliminated the word 'draw' from their vocabularies as they set about Sussex on the Monday morning, adding 182 for the 4th wicket and both reaching well-deserved hundreds. Bell in particular had done well for, since he had been omitted a year and a day previously

Tim Ambrose (85) put on 125 for the 7th wicket in Sussex's first innings against Warwickshire at Edgbaston.

from England's Test squad, his confidence had been eroded and he had spent much time concerned about perceived weaknesses in his technique. Some correspondents, however, took the view that any assessment of Bell and Troughton as Test prospects was unreal, so poorly had Sussex bowled and fielded and so defensive had been their field placing that no pressure whatsoever had been exerted on the batting side.

Giles declared the Warwickshire innings closed on 285 for seven wickets and set Sussex 341 to win. They were never within a shout of the total, especially as Melvyn Betts and Dougie Brown swung the ball under the heavy cloud cover and found the right length to exploit the uneven bounce. Cottey batted through 38 overs for his 55, but the rest of the batting, apart from a dogged little innings by Kirtley, was a woeful procession as they were dismissed for 106 in 43 overs, their lowest total since September 2000. It was twenty-one years since Sussex had won a Championship match at Edgbaston; they made no improvement in this match.

With one home win and two away defeats Sussex were at least being involved in 'result' matches, but the manner of their losses surely gave cause for concern. Peter Moores, Sussex's director of cricket, was not too downhearted when he spoke to *The Kent and Sussex Courier*: 'All three results were possible at the start of play. However, they bowled better and throughout the game they put a bit more in than we did and it is rare for me to say that. There is a lot of the season to go and we can come back strongly.'

Warwickshire (22 points) beat Sussex (7 points) by 234 runs.

Warwickshire CCC V Sussex CCC, at Edgbaston -- 9, 10, 11, 12 May 2003   40p

Warwickshire CCC

	First Innings				Second Innings		
1.T.FROST+		b Kirtley	37	(2)	c Prior	b Lewry	0
2.J.J.L.TROTT	c Montgomerie	b Mushtaq Ahmed	134	(1)	lbw	b Lewry	5
3.M.A.WAGH		b Mushtaq Ahmed	43		lbw	b Martin-Jenkins	38
4.I.R.BELL	c Prior	b Mushtaq Ahmed	3		lbw	b Davis	107
5.J.O.TROUGHTON	c Prior	b Kirtley	41		c sub	b Davis	105
6.D.P.OSTLER	lbw	b Mushtaq Ahmed	1			b Martin-Jenkins	7
7.D.R.BROWN	c Ambrose	b Mushtaq Ahmed	0		c Montgomerie	b Martin-Jenkins	0
8.A.F.GILES*	lbw	b Mushtaq Ahmed	22		not out		13
9.M.A.SHEIKH	not out		57				
10.M.M.BETTS	c Cottey	b Kirtley	20				
11.A.RICHARDSON		b Martin-Jenkins	47				
	(6b, 7lb, 4nb, 0w)	Extras	17		(8b, 2lb, 0nb, 0w)	Extras	10
		TOTAL	**422**			TOTAL	**285** for 7 dec

Fall of wickets

First Innings	1 - 86	2 - 194	3 - 198	4 - 233	5 - 239	6 - 239	7 - 269	8 - 307	9 - 348	10 - 422
Second Innings	1 - 5	2 - 18	3 - 64	4 - 246	5 - 271	6 - 271	7 - 285	8 -	9 -	10 -

Bowling Analysis

1st Innings	O	M	R	W	2nd Innings	O	M	R	W
LEWRY	11	2	41	0	KIRTLEY	14	2	48	0
KIRTLEY	30	4	107	3	LEWRY	9	1	51	2
MARTIN-JENKINS	6.3	1	46	1	MUSHTAQ AHMED	13	0	69	0
MUSHTAQ AHMED	48	7	157	6	MARTIN-JENKINS	13	3	57	3
DAVIS	22	7	58	0	DAVIS	9	0	50	2

Sussex CCC

	First Innings				Second Innings		
1.R.R.MONTGOMERIE	lbw	b Sheikh	41	(2)	lbw	b Betts	0
2.M.W.GOODWIN	c Troughton	b Sheikh	28	(1)	lbw	b Betts	10
3.P.A.COTTEY	c Frost	b Richardson	41		lbw	b Brown	55
4.C.J ADAMS*		b Sheikh	22			b Betts	0
5.T.R.AMBROSE (6)	lbw	b Sheikh	85		lbw	b Betts	0
6.R.S.C.MARTIN-JENKINS(7)	c Frost	b Brown	7			b Betts	11
7.M.J.PRIOR+ (8)	c Ostler	b Betts	84			b Brown	5
8.M.J.G.DAVIS (9)	c Frost	b Betts	1		lbw	b Brown	0
9.MUSHTAQ AHMED (10)	not out		2	(10)	not out		7
10.R.J.KIRTLEY (5)	c Brown	b Giles	31	(9)	c Frost	b Richardson	6
11.J.D.LEWRY		b Betts	1			b Brown	0
	(4b, 17lb, 2nb, 1w)	Extras	24		(5b, 7lb, 0nb, 0w)	Extras	12
		TOTAL	**367**			TOTAL	**106**

Fall of wickets

First Innings	1 - 67	2 - 74	3 - 116	4 - 165	5 - 216	6 - 235	7 - 360	8 - 364	9 - 364	10 - 367
Second Innings	1 - 12	2 - 17	3 - 21	4 - 21	5 - 37	6 - 43	7 - 43	8 - 82	9 - 106	10 - 106

Bowling Analysis

1st Innings	O	M	R	W	2nd Innings	O	M	R	W
BETTS	23.4	2	83	3	BETTS	13	2	43	5
RICHARDSON	29	12	65	1	RICHARDSON	13	6	19	1
BROWN	23	7	76	1	SHEIKH	6	2	15	0
SHEIKH	28	11	60	4	BROWN	9	4	17	4
GILES	23	5	60	1	GILES	2	2	0	0
	2	1	2	0					

* Captain   + Wicketkeeper   Umpires G.I.Burgess & I.J.Gould   Scorers D.E.Wainwright & J.F.Hartridge

Toss won by   Warwickshire, who elected to bat

Bonus Points	Warwickshire	8	Sussex	7	RESULT: Warwickshire won by 234 runs

Scoring of Points: (a) for a win, 14 points, plus any points scored in the first innings. (b) In a tie, each side to score seven points, plus any scored in the first innings. (c) In a draw match, each side to score 4 points, plus any points scored in the first innings. (d) If the scores are equal in a drawn match, the side batting in the fourth inning to score seven points, plus any points scored in the first innings. (e) First innings points (awarded only for the performance in the first 130 overs of each first innings, retained whatever the result of the match)
(i) A maximum of five batting points to be available as follows: 200-249 runs – 1 pts, 250-299 runs – 2 pts, 300-349 runs – 3 pts, 350-399 runs – 4 pts, 400 runs+ - 5pts.
(ii) A maximum of three bowling points to be available as follows: 3-5 wickets taken – 1 point, 6-8 wickets taken – 2 points, 9-10 wickets – 3 points.

Hours of Play: 1st, 2nd & 3rd days	11am – 6.30pm (minimum 104 overs)	Lunch 1.15pm – 1.55pm	Tea 4.10pm – 4.30pm	(Any alterations to playing hours
4th day	11am – 6.00pm (80 +16 overs)	Lunch 1.00pm – 1.40pm	Tea 3.40pm – 4.00pm	or intervals will be announced)

THE BOWLER AT THE PAVILION END IS INDICATED ON THE THWAITE SCOREBOARD BY THE FIGURE ON THE RIGHT

Opposite Matt Prior scored 84 brisk runs against
Warwickshire at Edgbaston in early May.

SUSSEX v. NOTTINGHAMSHIRE AT HORSHAM

Wednesday to Saturday, 21 to 24 May, 2003

Having lost ignominiously to Warwickshire at Edgbaston, Sussex must have come with a little trepidation to Cricket Field Road, Horsham, to take on Nottinghamshire, who like Middlesex, victors over the County at Lord's, had been promoted from Division Two the previous season. On winning the toss and feeling the chill in the air, Chris Adams had no difficulty in deciding to take first use of a good pitch on this picturesque ground overlooked by Horsham parish church at the north end and hardly aware of the railway at the other.

While it is true that Sussex openers Richard Montgomerie and Murray Goodwin did not in 2002 quite replicate the magnificent season they had enjoyed the previous year when the County had been promoted, they remain an excellent pair and were soon about their business. In fact, they added 87 in 21 overs before Goodwin edged Elworthy, the best of the Notts seamers, to Pietersen at third slip. In strode Tony Cottey, who thus far had not made any significant mark on Sussex's totals, but now he batted with typical Welsh determination and common sense and added 123 for the 2nd wicket with Montgomerie. He then hoisted his half-century by taking two fours off Stuart MacGill, the Australian Test bowler just back from Antigua, who obligingly provided a long hop outside the off stump followed by a knee-high full toss outside the leg stump. That was it, however, as Cottey soon failed to spot MacGill's googly and padded up and was adjudged lbw.

Montgomerie clearly likes batting at Horsham and, in the course of the afternoon, he went on to his hundred off 185 balls, his third in succession on the ground and the fourth in seven innings against Notts. MacGill, once he gets on in county cricket, normally finds himself bowling non-stop and this innings was no different. Despite some further erratic deliveries he had captured three of the first four wickets, but then he was put to the sword by Robin Martin-Jenkins, who in a run-a-ball 49 struck some sumptuous shots before holing out to deep square leg off Andrew Harris. With 18 overs still to be bowled, umpires Cowley and Llong conferred and offered the light, although some thought that it was the cold which made them seek the shelter of the pavilion. Sussex, however, with young guns Tim Ambrose and Matt Prior both not out, were undoubtedly pleased with their 330 for five wickets, scored at nearly four runs an over.

The Thursday morning was bright but a chill wind blew hard and buffeted Neil Beck's book table and the club's open-sided caravan which serves as a shop at matches away from Hove. Ambrose reached his fifty before being taken at the wicket and Prior was then joined by Kevin Innes who enjoyed a remarkable and fulfilling day. James Kirtley was in the England squad for the Lord's Test against Zimbabwe but, in the event, he was omitted from the side. An ECB regulation introduced in 2003 stipulates that players released from the England squad can return to their county and replace previously nominated players, even if that player has already contributed with bat or ball. The fact that the start of the Test was slightly delayed meant that Kirtley, who was a two-hour drive away from Horsham, had not arrived before Innes went out to bat. Prior played the leading role in a feast of runs before lunch as the pair added 157 in 27 overs. In the morning session he scored 124 runs with 15 fours and six sixes, pulling Bilal Shafayat

Richard Montgomerie plays forward against Nottinghamshire at Horsham towards the end of May as England wicketkeeper, Chris Read, looks on.

for six to reach his hundred and, in fact, speeding from 98 to 133 off the last 11 balls he received before the lunch interval. One six off Kevin Pietersen was a massive hit over square leg on the side opposite the pavilion and cleared the albeit shortish boundary by miles.

Prior holed out at deep extra cover immediately after the interval to conclude a 146-ball innings of great precision of shot and tremendous power. Innes, however, now in partnership with Mark Davis, was not to be denied. Dropped on 45, he otherwise needed very little luck, striking 14 fours and two sixes and dancing with joy when he pulled a boundary off Pietersen to reach his maiden first-class hundred. At a quarter past three Sussex had reached the highest score on the Horsham ground and Adams applied the closure. Innes had become the first 'twelfth man' to score a first-class hundred and, as Notts went out to score 470 to avoid the follow-on, he was transformed, Cinderella-like, from batting hero to drinks waiter. Guy Welton and Jason Gallian added 71 for Notts' 1st wicket before the latter was caught by Prior down the leg side off Billy Taylor. With the score on 85 for one wicket off 24 overs, bad light brought the proceedings to an end for the second day an hour earlier than one would have wished.

The Friday almost belonged to Nottinghamshire's young batting hopefuls, but not quite. Welton added only five to his overnight score before being pinned on the back foot by Mushtaq and, although Afzaal made a bustling 35, four Notts wickets were down for 139 when Shafayat joined Pietersen. Both are seen as England Test prospects: Pietersen, born in 1980 in South Africa but England-qualified through parentage, will be available for selection midway through the 2004 season, while the eighteen-year-old Shafayat, who has led the England Under-19 XI, has been talked about as a Test player for a year or so, although prematurely, if the Notts coach, Mick Newell, is to be believed. On this day the pair exhibited their wares fully, bludgeoning 193 runs for the 5th wicket in a display of huge audacity. When Pietersen was stumped for 166 by Ambrose, standing in for the injured Prior, he had faced a mere 136 balls and had hit 17 fours and four sixes, having reached his hundred off only 75 balls, two adrift of the season's fastest. Shafayat, all timing and touch, proceeded to 71, lifting Mushtaq for two straight sixes before falling to the Pakistani's wiles. Sussex, however, achieved their target by causing the visitors to follow on, but their bowling had taken a pummelling, Mushtaq going for 163 runs in claiming his six wickets and Kirtley, having been hit straight for six by Pietersen, decided to try some 'throat balls' and was struck for three fours and a six in the course of six balls. Notts, with Darren Bicknell, still aided by a runner on account of a calf strain, joining Gallian at the top of the order, topped the hundred before the close and looked like saving the match with comfort. Mushtaq, fielding disconsolately on the third-man boundary, described the pitch as 'very slow.'

What Notts should have achieved with ease by batting through the day and saving the match, they signally failed to do. In the course of 48 overs they lost all ten wickets for 144 runs on a pitch which was probably playing better than it had done throughout the match, and went down to a ten-wicket defeat. The opening pair went quickly,

Tony Cottey pushes a single past Guy Welton (Notts) at Horsham.

Above left Mushtaq bowls against Nottinghamshire at Horsham. *Above right* No greater pleasure than a wicket! Mushtaq sees the departure of another Nottinghamshire batsman.

Below left Kevin Innes acknowledges his century, the first ever scored by a twelfth man under the new ECB regulations. *Below right* Kevin Innes poses in front of the Horsham scoreboard.

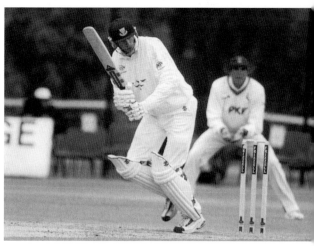

Left Tony Cottey hooks to the boundary in the course of his 58 against Nottinghamshire at Horsham.

Below Robin Martin-Jenkins turns a ball to leg in his innings against Kent at Nottinghamshire at Horsham.

Bicknell to a brilliant caught-and-bowled by Kirtley and Gallian to a bat-pad catch off Mushtaq. Worse was to follow: six wickets were down for 143, Pietersen held at slip for a single and Shafayat bowled middle stump by a googly for one fewer, both to Mushtaq. Adams was ecstatic about his Pakistani leg-spinner: 'The delivery which got Shafayat was something Shane Warne would have been proud of,' he said. A 7th-wicket stand of 94 in 24 overs between Chris Read and Steve Elworthy temporarily stopped the rot, but the end was in sight and the last four wickets went down for the addition of ten runs. Needing 49 to win Sussex made light of the task, Goodwin striking Harris for six to end the match just before tea.

Mushtaq had been brought into the Sussex set-up in 2003 to provide a penetrative spin factor to go with Kirtley's pace and, in fact, by taking 12 wickets for 244 in this match, he became the first Sussex spinner since Ian Salisbury in 1996 to take ten wickets in a match. Both bowlers harbour Test ambitions. Mushtaq said after the match: 'If the Pakistan selectors are honest then I think I should be in the Test side', while Kirtley, perhaps disappointed by his rejection by England at Lord's, responded positively at Horsham and, as the only English bowler to take 50 first-class wickets in each of the previous five seasons, moved confidently towards another half-century.

Peter Moores, director of cricket at Sussex, talking to *The Kent and Sussex Courier*, was especially pleased as Sussex moved into third place in the Championship table: 'It was a fantastic performance, especially after the Warwickshire defeat. From the start we outplayed them and everybody contributed. Before the game we had not had a Championship century and to register three at Horsham was great.'

Sussex (22 points) beat Nottinghamshire (7 points) by ten wickets.

SUSSEX v NOTTINGHAMSHIRE

at Horsham on 21st - 24th May - Frizzell County Championship Division 1

Sussex won the toss and elected to bat

* Captain, + Wicket-Keeper

SUSSEX

		1st Innings		2nd Innings	
1	R.R. Montgomerie [7]	c: Gallian b: MacGill	105	not out	25
2	M.W. Goodwin [3]	c: Pietersen b: Elworthy	38	not out	23
3	P.A. Cottey [2]	Lbw b: MacGill	58		
4	C.J. Adams * [1]	c: Gallian b: MacGill	9		
5	T.R. Ambrose [11]	c: Read b: Elworthy	55		
6	R.S.C. Martin-Jenkins [12]	c: Welton b: Harris	49		
7	M.J. Prior + [13]	c: sub b: Elworthy	133		
8	K.J. Innes [15]	not out	103		
9	M.J.G. Davis [8]	not out	32		
10	Mushtaq Ahmed [9]				
11	B.V. Taylor [22]				
12	R.J. Kirtley [6]				

b 2	lb 20	wd 1	nb 14	Extras	37	b 0	lb 2	wd 0	nb 2	Extras	4
Overs	147		Provisional Total		619	Overs	0		Provisional Total		52
Pens	0	Wkts	7 decl	Total	619	Pens	10.2	Wkts	0	Total	52

Fall of 1st Inns: 1 - 87   2 - 210   3 - 227   4 - 232   5 - 312   6 - 378   7 - 535
wickets

Bonus Points -   Sussex 5, Notts 2

Bowling	Ovs	Md	R	Wk	wd	nb	Ovs	Md	R	Wk	wd	nb
Smith	24	2	97	0	0	2	-	-	-	-	-	-
Harris	20	2	102	1	0	5	0.2	0	6	0	0	0
Gallian	12	2	45	0	0	0	-	-	-	-	-	-
Elworthy	30	3	107	3	1	0	5	1	22	0	0	0
MacGill	50	12	172	3	0	0	4	1	13	0	0	0
Shafayat	4	0	39	0	0	0	-	-	-	-	-	-
Pietersen	7	0	35	0	0	0	1	0	9	0	0	1

NOTTS

		1st Innings		2nd Innings (Following-on / 198 behind)	
1	G.E. Welton [19]	Lbw b: Mushtaq	50	(3) st: Ambrose b: Mushtaq	12
2	J.E.R. Gallian * [1]	c: Prior b: Taylor	36	c: Montgomerie b: Mushtaq	44
3	U. Afzaal [4]	c: Ambrose b: Kirtley	35	(4) c: Ambrose b: Kirtley	18
4	D.J. Bicknell [2]	Lbw b: Kirtley	9	(1) ct & b: Kirtley	61
5	K.P. Pietersen [6]	st: Ambrose b: Mushtaq	166	c: Cottey b: Mushtaq	1
6	B.M. Shafayat [14]	Lbw b: Mushtaq	71	b: Mushtaq	0
7	C.M.W. Read + [7]	Lbw b: Mushtaq	0	Lbw b: Mushtaq	42
8	S. Elworthy [21]	c: Ambrose b: Martin-Jenkins	28	c: Ambrose b: Mushtaq	45
9	G.J. Smith [9]	b: Mushtaq	9	not out	5
10	A.J. Harris [13]	b: Mushtaq	5	st: Ambrose b: Mushtaq	1
11	S.C.G. MacGill [3]	not out	4	c: Sub (Innes) b: Kirtley	2
12	M. Footitt				

b 1	lb 1	wd 0	nb 6	Extras	8	b 0	lb 5	wd 1	nb 10	Extras	16
Overs	93.1		Provisional Total		421	Overs	82.2		Provisional Total		247
Pens	0	Wkts	10	Total	421	Pens	0	Wkts	10	Total	247

Fall of   1st Inns: 1 - 71   2 - 109   3 - 126   4 - 139   5 - 332   6 - 332   7 - 369   8 - 390   9 - 398   10 - 421
wickets   2nd Inns: 1 - 103   2 - 111   3 - 132   4 - 133   5 - 142   6 - 143   7 - 237   8 - 239   9 - 242   10 - 247

Bonus Points -   Notts 5, Sussex 3

Bowling	Ovs	Md	R	Wk	wd	nb	Ovs	Md	R	Wk	wd	nb
Kirtley	21	7	85	2	0	1	24.2	4	74	4	1	3
Martin-Jenkins	17	0	87	1	0	0	6	1	25	0	0	0
Mushtaq Ahmed	37.1	3	163	6	0	2	30	9	81	6	0	0
Taylor	11	3	32	1	0	0	13	3	36	0	0	2
Davis	7	0	52	0	0	0	9	1	26	0	0	0

SUSSEX WON BY 10 WKTS

CLUB SPONSORS
2003
OFFICIAL CLUB
SPONSOR:
P@v - i.t. services
SPONSORS:
ACCELERATED MAILING
ALLFIELD FINANCIAL GROUP
BAKER TILLY
CHARCOL
ERADICATION & CLEANING
FAMILY ASSURANCE
FINN CRISP
GILES CONTRACTS MGMT LTD
GRAND CRU GROUP
MISHON MACKAY
PSE ASSOCIATES
RENDEZVOUS CASINO
RIVERVALE
SETYRES
SHEPHERD NEAME
SOLV IT
TATES
THE SUPPORTERS CLUB
VOKINS @ HOME
WYNDEHAM PRESS GRP
WYNNE BAXTER

UMPIRES :
N.G. Cowley
N.J. Llong
SCORERS :
J.F. Hartridge
G. Stringfellow

HOURS OF PLAY
Days 1 - 3: 11am - 6.30pm
Day 4 : 11am - 6pm
Lunch
Days 1 - 3: 1.15pm - 1.55pm
Day 4 : 1pm - 1.40pm
Tea
Days 1 - 3 : 4.10pm - 4.30pm
or when 32 overs remain to
be bowled, whichever is later
Day 4 : 3.40pm - 4pm
1st Inns Bonus Pts
(Only in the first 130 Overs)
Batting (Max 5pts)
1pt at achieving 200, 250,
300, 350 and 400 runs.
Bowling (Max 3pts)
1 pt for taking 3, 6 & 9 wkts

43

SUSSEX v. SURREY AT THE AMP OVAL

Friday to Monday, 30 May to 2 June 2003

Surrey, with their immense list of Test players, looked from the start of the season to be in a strong position to retain the Championship they had won in 2002 and in three of the past four years. It would have been bold to bet very much against them and their early season form was good.

Adam Hollioake, when he won the toss, doubtless had little difficulty in deciding to bat on an excellent Oval pitch but, perversely perhaps, Surrey made a wobbly start against the new-ball bowling of James Kirtley and Billy Taylor. Openers Ian Ward and Jon Batty were both back in the pavilion by the 10th over when there were only 22 runs on the board. Both men will have different roles in 2004 – Ward will join Sussex's own ranks, while Batty has been selected to replace Hollioake as Surrey's skipper. This means, presumably, that he will bat lower down the order as captaining, opening and keeping wicket are always likely to be too much for any one man. Alec Stewart will doubtless have been able to tell him all about that scenario.

It was incumbent, therefore, upon Mark Ramprakash and Graham Thorpe to steady the Surrey ship and, by taking stock of the situation, they did precisely that. Thorpe, back in the Surrey side now that the England men had departed for higher things (what luxury to have a batter of his ability in the reserves!) eventually started to take the lead role, while Ramprakash, still with probably the best technique in England, but with little appetite for the world stage, managed just one scoring stroke from his first 51 balls. After they had added 110 in 36 overs he departed for 37, which brought in the ebullient Ali Brown who clubbed 74 with 11 fours and a six. The pressure was now off Surrey as Taylor had limped off after seven overs with a thigh strain. His replacement, Robin Martin-Jenkins, was disappointingly wayward by comparison, and Thorpe and Brown had no difficulty in dispatching some over-pitched balls to distant parts of the large arena. The latter's departure saw the arrival of the Surrey skipper who settled in easily into Brown's role. After tea Mushtaq, a guest replacement player for Surrey in 2002, who had wheeled away with only the wicket of Ramprakash to his credit, at last managed to deceive Thorpe, who cut him to Adams at backward point. The left-hander's innings had lasted for five hours and 25 minutes and he had faced 274 balls of which 26 had found their way to the boundary. Kevin Innes's lack of pace had made him largely ineffective, and it was left to Kirtley to bear the brunt of the Sussex attack with Martin-Jenkins, who accounted for Hollioake for 77, and to reduce the hosts to eight wickets down. For all that, however, with five batting points in the bag and two wickets remaining, Surrey must have felt that they had had a good day.

Surrey had, of course, by no means finished on their overnight 401 for eight wickets. They bat a long way down, and Ian Salisbury and Saqlain Mushtaq, both with first-class hundreds to their name, added 75 for the 9th wicket on the Saturday morning before they were all out. In that time they had taken toll of a slightly demoralised Sussex attack where 17 overs bar one ball had gone for 70 runs and Kirtley had been hoisted by Saqlain into the pavilion.

Opposite Mike Yardy almost held on for a draw against Surrey at The Oval at the end of May and the beginning of June.

Many critics believe that Jimmy Ormond, Surrey's opening bowler, would, but for his easy-going attitude and apparent failure to reach the fitness standards demanded by England's Duncan Fletcher, be in front of Kirtley and Johnson of Somerset in the Test pecking order. He is, however, a formidable competitor on the county scene and, when Sussex came to bat, he soon sent back Richard Montgomerie, caught at cover off a mispull, and Michael Yardy, caught at third slip. When skipper Chris Adams, in the mode where he scarcely moves his feet and hacks the ball with short-arm drives, was caught by the wicketkeeper from a skier off Azhar Mahmood, Sussex were in the doldrums at 24 for three wickets. Luckily for them, Murray Goodwin, recognising The Oval pitch to be as good as that at the WACA where he plays his winter cricket, was in top form and made 60 off 66 balls before a fastish off-break from Saqlain went through his defence. The rest of the Sussex innings was held together by Tim Ambrose, determinedly, and by Robin Martin-Jenkins, adventurously, but even though Mushtaq batted in his own cheeky style for 41 the eventual total of 307 reached had not avoided the follow-on.

With a lead of 173 Hollioake might well have invited Sussex to bat again, but owing to the heat and the fact that Martin Bicknell had strained a hamstring, he decided to go in again, Surrey reaching 22 for no wicket by the close. The omens, however, were clearly in favour of a Surrey victory, but Hollioake had not perhaps thought hard about the weather. What he clearly had in mind at the start was to bat Sussex out of the game and then declare and look for wickets in the last session of the third day. As things panned out, Ward helped himself to a second Championship hundred of the season while Batty reached 50, but the weather closed in during the afternoon and Surrey's lead was only 406 when Hollioake decided he had to act. With a possible 13 overs remaining he put Sussex back in, but he was again frustrated as only 3.5 overs could be completed as his opponents moved to 12 without loss.

The final day, the Monday, was to prove a day of attrition, although at the outset it was not clear whether Sussex were going for broke and trying to reach 407 for victory. There must have been long odds on their achieving this total, but when Goodwin was bowled trying to pull Azhar through mid-wicket and Montgomerie, Adams and Ambrose all disappeared in a Saqlain spell of three wickets while two runs were added, they clearly settled for a draw. Michael Yardy, who had come into the side owing to Tony Cottey's back injury and was batting at number 3 for the first time in his career, dropped anchor, while Martin-Jenkins continued in his fluent form of the first innings. In fact, Yardy contributed a mere 19 runs to the 5th-wicket partnership of 113 as his partner sped to 88 with 14 boundaries off 92 balls. Prior and Innes made little contribution, but Kirtley stayed doggedly for 11 overs in Yardy's company. After that Mushtaq batted again in the only way he knows how before he tried to hit his fellow Pakistani out of The Oval. This brought in last man Billy Taylor, and Hollioake called up all ten fielders to lurk under his nose. Strangely, however, it was Yardy who was dismissed. Having batted with great application for five hours, he edged Ormond with the new ball to second slip and Surrey had won. Tantalisingly, there were just 5.2 overs remaining.

Surrey (22 points) beat Sussex (6 points) by 113 runs.

SURREY COUNTY CRICKET CLUB

v Sussex County Cricket Club
at The AMP Oval
Friday 30th May – Monday 2nd June 2003
Umpires A. A. Jones & R. Palmer
Scorers K. R. Booth & J. F. Hartridge

For the latest news about Surrey County Cricket Club go online at www.surreycricket.com
Toss Won By:- Surrey who elected to bat
Result:- Surrey won by 113 runs
*Captain   +Wicketkeeper   30p

Surrey

Batsman	1st Innings		2nd Innings	
1. I. J. Ward	c Ambrose b Kirtley	9	c Goodwin b Innes	135
2. J. N. Batty+	c Adams b Taylor	12	b Mushtaq Ahmed	56
3. M.R. Ramprakash	c Yardy b Mushtaq Ahmed	37	c Prior b Innes	23
4. G. P. Thorpe	c Adams b Mushtaq Ahmed	156	not out	18
5. A. D Brown	c Goodwin b Kirtley	74	not out	1
6. A. J. Hollioake*	lbw b Martin-Jenkins	77		
7. Azhar Mahmood	c Adams b Kirtley	0		
8. M. P. Bicknell	b Martin-Jenkins	11		
9. I.D.K. Salisbury	c Ambrose b M. Ahmed	45		
10. Saqlain Mushtaq	c Montgomerie b Jenkins	32		
11. J. Ormond	not out	1		
Extras	b 4 lb 17 w 1 nb 4	26	b lb w nb	0
Total	all out 119.5 overs	480	3 wkts dec 60 overs	233

Fall of Wickets

1st Innings: 1-22 2-22 3-132 4-263 5-359 6-360 7-379 8-394 9-469 10-480

2nd Innings: 1-137 2-195 3-219 4- 5- 6- 7- 8- 9- 10-

Sussex Bowling

1st Innings	O	M	R	W	Wd	Nb
Kirtley	33	5	122	3		2
Taylor	7.2	2	15	1		
M-Jenkins	23.4	8	86	3		1
Innes	12	4	59	0		
M.Ahmed	36.5	1	159	3		
Yardy	7	1	18	0		

2nd Innings	O	M	R	W	Wd	Nb
Kirtley	14	3	49	0		
M-Jenkins	19	3	66	0		
M.Ahmed	11	1	47	2		
Innes	14	1	64	2		
Yardy	2	0	7	0		

Sussex

Batsman	1st Innings		2nd Innings	
1. R. R. Montgomerie (7)	c Ward b Ormond	5	c Sub b Mushtaq	31
2. M. W. Goodwin (3)	b Saqlain Mushtaq	60	b Azhar Mahmood	26
3. M. H. Yardy (20)	c Thorpe b Ormond	0	c Mahmood b Ormond	69
4. C. J. Adams* (1)	c Batty b Mahmood	5	b Saqlain Mushtaq	0
5. T. R. Ambrose (11)	C Ramprakash b Ormond	75	b Saqlain Mushtaq	1
6. R.S.C. Martin-Jenkins (12)	lbw b Mahmood	61	b Azhar Mahmood	88
7. M. J. Prior+ (13)	b Saqlain Mushtaq	6	c Ramprakash b Mahmood	14
8. K. J. Innes (15)	b Salisbury	2	c Mahmood b Mushtaq	1
9. Mushtaq Ahmed (9)	lbw b Ormond	41	lbw Saqlain Mushtaq	36
10. R. J. Kirtley (6)	run out	21	c Sub b Salisbury	7
11. B. V. Taylor (22)	not out	4	not out	0
Extras	lb 9 w 2 nb 16	27	b 9 lb 3 w 2 nb 6	20
Total	all out 73.1 overs	307	all out 95.4 overs	293

Fall of Wickets

1st Innings: 1-5 2-13 3-24 4-98 5-189 6-217 7-220 8-279 9-282 10-307

2nd Innings: 1-45 2-83 3-83 4-85 5-198 6-218 7-221 8-242 9-293 10-293

Surrey Bowling

1st Innings	O	M	R	W	Wd	Nb
Bicknell	3	1	9	0		
Ormond	15.1	2	81	4		5
A. Mahmood	16	1	57	1		
Salisbury	14	1	67	1		3
S. Mushtaq	21	4	68	2		
Hollioake	4	0	16	0		

2nd Innings	O	M	R	W	Wd	Nb
Ormond	19.4	3	63	1	2	
A.Mahmood	21	5	76	3		
Salisbury	21	5	67	1		
S.Mushtaq	34	15	73	5		1

SUSSEX v. KENT AT TUNBRIDGE WELLS
Wednesday to Saturday, 4 to 7 June 2003

The Nevill Ground in Tunbridge Wells is among the most attractive in England, especially when on three of its sides the rhododendrons are in bloom. The town values its first-class cricket, which is now restricted, of course, to one Championship match since the inception of the four-day game. The white marquees on the town side for the benefit of the mayor and his many guests, the Lord Lieutenant, the cricket clubs and the firms offering corporate hospitality are matched by smaller tents and stalls on the opposite side. All this splendid show contributes greatly to the festival atmosphere. But that is very much the upside; the downside is the fact that the practice field is often too soggy to act as a car-park and that the local council stations bollards all along the roads outside, which means that the local taxis have a field day. Perhaps more important, however, is the fact that the Nevill possesses what cricketers know as a 'result' pitch. Any tactical error, any lapse in cricketing skill and, frankly, any piece of bad luck can have the direst consequences for the unlucky team.

There had been some rain overnight and, when the teams and the many guests and spectators arrived at the Nevill, the sky was still grey and fitful bursts of rain, some quite heavy, dampened spirits. Unhelpful pools of water lay on the covers and on the outfield as gentlemen in panamas and ladies in high heels made their way along the temporary metal track, more reminiscent of a makeshift airfield in Second World War Burma than a cricket field, to the marquees where spirits of a different sort were on hand to console the would-be spectators.

After lunch the sky lightened and prodigious efforts by the ground staff meant that play was able to get under way at 3.45 p.m., but 60 overs had been lost by this time. Even the start was not without incident, the public address first announcing that Kent had won the toss and put Sussex in, then it corrected itself to say that Kent would bat, only for a third attempt to give the facts – Sussex had won the toss and would take first use of the pitch. Alamgir Sheriyar, who had bowled well in Sussex's home match at Hove on the last day of April and the first days of May, was again on song and Richard Montgomerie, trying to withdraw his bat, allowed the ball to hit it and played on, while Tony Cottey shuffled across and was palpably lbw for nought. Murray Goodwin was timing the ball well and, in company with Chris Adams, added 54 before the former, responding to his captain's call, was run out by Martin Saggers. After Ambrose had been tamely caught at third slip, Adams started to assert himself, driving firmly down the ground and hitting 11 fours from 76 balls before he too perished, caught in the gully. With Sussex on 142 for five wickets from 44 overs at the close, neither side can have felt especially pleased with the day's work.

The Thursday morning was much brighter and Sussex batted on in fine style. Robin Martin-Jenkins, in something of a purple patch, continued sensibly with the stubborn assistance of nightwatchman Paul Hutchison and reached his third consecutive half-century before pulling a long-hop to mid-wicket. With the help of the tail the Sussex

Opposite Matt Prior, resplendent in a 'Sharks' helmet, scores against Kent.

total finally reached the third hundred and with it three batting points – probably a reasonable result in view of the conditions on the previous day.

Between the innings James Kirtley, discarded for a second time in a fortnight from England's ranks, arrived at the ground from the Riverside ground in Durham, but needed time to get himself ready for the fray. In the circumstances, Hutchison, the player nominated to be replaced under the new ECB regulations, went out and opened the bowling with Jason Lewry. It almost seemed as if Sussex were pushing their luck a little with this ploy, but he conceded 27 runs in five overs before Kirtley joined the party. The Kent openers, Greg Blewett and Michael Carberry, batted sensibly until the latter sliced a ball to the gully off the England discard just before tea. After the interval Kirtley trapped Ed Smith in front and Kevin Innes's medium pace saw Blewett play defensively and see the ball trickle back and remove a bail. The pitch now seemed to have lost some of its life and Andrew Symonds and Matthew Walker batted serenely in a 90-run partnership before the wiles of Mushtaq forced the Australian to sky to long off and Walker to be snapped up by Ambrose off bat and pad.

Mushtaq was feeling distinctly below par when play began on the Friday morning but, mainly in harness with Kirtley, he started to unravel the Kent innings despite his need to call for water and medication during the innings. He quickly disposed of Alex Loudon and acting captain Mark Ealham and, although Geraint Jones, batting rather low at number 8, scored an unbeaten 46 off 38 balls, including two straight sixes off Mushtaq, the rest of the Kent batting folded to give Sussex a modest lead of 36.

Saggers trapped Montgomerie in front with the third ball of Sussex's second innings, but Goodwin and Cottey added 111 for the 2nd wicket before the latter tried to work Symonds to leg and was lbw. Not long afterwards Goodwin, seemingly impervious to the Kent attack, self-destructed as he called Adams for a cheeky single, was sent back and run out for the second time in the match. Both Cottey and he had struck eight fours in their particularly well-constructed half-centuries. With Adams and Ambrose bringing the lbw victims to four out of the five wickets that had fallen, Martin-Jenkins again took charge, playing beautifully off his legs and through mid-on, and was five short of another 50 when the close came with Sussex on 188 for five wickets. A lead of 224 with five wickets left seemed to show Sussex to be ahead, but much was going to depend on how Mushtaq came through the night after he had repaired immediately at the close of play to his darkened room in the Royal Wells Inn, the team hotel. The final day had all the makings of something dramatic.

Mushtaq, recovered through the ministrations of the Kent doctor, was able to take his place in the Sussex line-up on the Saturday morning as Martin-Jenkins and Matthew Prior added 89 for the 6th wicket and began to emphasise Sussex's superiority. Martin-Jenkins was again in prime form and completed his fourth half-century on the trot meaning he had obtained, incidentally the Sussex top score from the number 6 berth in three consecutive innings, before he edged behind after taking a mere 92 balls for his 84, which included 11 fours and a six. Prior's 45 was a small foretaste of what he would offer later in the season and, when the Sussex innings ended on 286, they had set Kent 323 to win – the highest total of the match.

Lewry straight away had Blewett taken at the wicket, but Carberry and Smith both batted with supreme confidence, driving straight down the ground with considerable

Above left Murray Goodwin, despite being run out in both innings against Kent at Tunbridge Wells, also made some runs. *Right* Chris Adams and Murray Goodwin discuss their tactics in dealing with the Kent bowling.

Below left The long and the short of it. Robin Martin-Jenkins and Tim Ambrose confer at Tunbridge Wells. *Right* Jason Lewry wields a heavy bat.

power, until Mushtaq was brought on by Adams one over before lunch and left to bowl while the seamers were rotated at the other end. Mushtaq so bemused Carberry that he found himself halfway down the track on all fours with his leg bail missing. Smith then immediately edged Lewry to slip, whereupon Mushtaq had Symonds lbw for a single as he failed to offer a stroke to the googly. Martin-Jenkins promptly stepped in and completed a wholly excellent all-round performance by taking three quick wickets. When Mushtaq cleaned up the tail he had taken nine wickets in the match and had become the season's leading wicket taker, as Kent subsided to 131 all out – a double defeat at the hands of Sussex – and a loss by the substantial margin of 191 runs.

Robin Martin-Jenkins, speaking to *The Argus*, said that he could not remember a time when he had batted so consistently for the County and added: 'My bowling hasn't been great, but in the last two weeks my rhythm has come back. I felt I was putting more balls

Mushtaq made a useful 43 against Kent at Tunbridge Wells.

KENT

1st Innings			2nd Innings	
1	G Blewett	b Innes	46	c Prior b Lewry	0
2	M A Carberry	c Cottey b Kirtley	23	b Mushtaq Ahmed	40
3	E T Smith	lbw Kirtley	13	c Montgomerie b Lewry	40
4	A Symonds	c Innes b Mushtaq	54	lbw b Mushtaq Ahmed	1
5	M J Walker	c Ambrose b Mushtaq	30	c Prior b Lewry	7
*6	M A Ealham (7)	c Martin-Jenkins b Mushtaq	9	lbw b Martin-Jenkins	3
+7	G O Jones (8)	not out	46	c Lewry b Martin-Jenkins	22
8	J C Tredwell (9)	lbw b Kirtley	16	c Montgomerie b Mushtaq Ahmed	11
9	M J Saggers (10)	b Kirtley	2	not out	0
10	A Sheriyar (11)	lbw b Mushtaq	7	c Goodwin b Mushtaq Ahmed	4
11	A J R Loudon (6)	c Ambrose b Mushtaq	8	lbw b Martin-Jenkins	0
12	B J Trott				

Extras B - 11 L/B - 10 W - 0 NB - 0   **21** B - 0 L/B - 1 W - 2 NB - 0   **3**

Total - 275   Total - 131

Runs at fall of wicket

	1	2	3	4	5	6	7	8	9	10
1st Innings	1-74	2-84	3-90	4-180	5-180	6-198	7-203	8-238	9-250	10-27
2nd Innings	1-0	2-65	3-66	4-83	5-99	6-110	7-127	8-127	9-	10-

Bowling Analysis	Overs	Maidens	Runs	Wickets	Bowling Analysis	Overs	Maidens	Runs	Wickets
Lewry	11	4	19	0	Kirtley	9	2	29	0
Hutchison	5	0	27	0	Lewry	11	2	36	3
Martin-Jenkins	10	3	26	0	Ahmed Mushtaq	20.4	7	56	4
Kirtley	21	4	84	4	Martin-Jenkins	7	3	9	3
Innes	9	1	28	1					
Mushtaq	17.2	3	70	5					

SUSSEX

1st Innings			2nd Innings	
1	R R Montgomerie 7	b Sheriyar	13	lbw b Saggers	0
2	M W Goodwin 3	run out	35	run out	58
3	P A Cottey 2	lbw b Sheriyar	0	lbw b Symonds	52
*4	C J Adams 1	c Ealham b Sheriyar	62	lbw b Sheriyar	4
5	T R Ambrose 11	c Walker b Blewett	11	lbw b Symonds	17
6	R Martin-Jenkins 12	c Tredwell b Symonds	67	c Jones b Sheriyar	84
+7	M J Prior 13 (8)	c Symonds b Saggers	23	c & b Tredwell	45
8	K J Innes 15 (9)	c and b Sheriyar	30	b Tredwell	0
9	P M Hutchison (7)	b Ealham	18	c Loudon b Sheriyar	9
10	Mushtaq Ahmed 9	c Jones b Saggers	43	not out	1
11	J D Lewry 5	not out	0	c Jones b Sheriyar	0
12	R J Kirtley 6				

Extras B - 2 L/B - 5 W - 2 NB - 0   **9** B - 3 L/B 12 W - 1 NB - 0   **16**

Total - 311   Total - 286

Runs at fall of wicket

	1	2	3	4	5	6	7	8	9	10
1st Innings	1-21	2-25	3-79	4-104	5-136	6-174	7-205	8-249	9-311	10-31
2nd Innings	1-1	2-112	3-117	4-131	5-184	6-273	7-284	8-285	9-286	10-

Bowling Analysis	Overs	Maidens	Runs	Wickets	Bowling Analysis	Overs	Maidens	Runs	Wickets
Saggers	24.1	6	76	2	Saggers	20	4	62	1
Sheriyar	24	6	49	4	Sheriyar	23.5	1	93	4
Ealham	20	8	63	1	Ealham	10	2	37	0
Blewett	5	0	21	1	Symonds	10	1	25	2
Tredwell	12	0	65	0	Tredwell	10	2	37	2
Symonds	10	2	30	1	Blewett	2	0	17	0

in the right areas, so I knew it was a matter of time before wickets would come and hopefully that will continue for the rest of the season.' Robin noted finally that he saw Surrey as the best side in the Championship, but believed that Sussex did not need to fear any other county.

Sussex (20 points) beat Kent (5 points) by 191 runs.

SUSSEX v. WARWICKSHIRE AT HOVE

Friday to Sunday, 27 to 29 June 2003

Sussex had unpleasant memories of their last encounter with Warwickshire when, to the muted horror of their captain and director of cricket, they had crashed to an ignominious defeat at Edgbaston in early May. Now that the Twenty20 Cup had come and gone and cricket was back to the serious stuff of the Championship, matters needed to be different, but Sussex were at least able to say that they had so far in the season recorded three wins against the Midlanders' one.

The Hove pitches nowadays are usually top-rate for batting, thanks to the efforts of Derek Traill and his staff, and this Friday morning in June was no exception. Chris Adams won the toss and chose to take first use of the splendid track. Although Murray Goodwin flicked a leg-side delivery from Waqar Younis into the waiting hands of the wicketkeeper in the very first over, that was all the success the Warwickshire bowlers enjoyed in the first session. Richard Montgomerie and Tony Cottey found little difficulty in dealing with their opponents' attack, despite the two international bowlers – Waqar Younis of Pakistan via Surrey and Glamorgan and the emerging young Kenyan leg-spinner, Collins Obuya – in their ranks. In fact, Waqar is not the terror of old and Obuya is still very much a novice at first-class level and the two Sussex batsmen prospered as too much that was short and wide was served up to them.

Montgomerie perished after the pair had added 165 runs for the 2nd wicket when, attempting to pull Dougie Brown, he top-edged to Tony Frost behind the stumps, having recorded only his second Championship 50 thus far in the season. Not long afterwards Cottey came to his first-ever hundred at Hove in the early afternoon, having hit ten fours along the way, although he slowed a little in the 90s and survived a difficult chance to Mark Wagh at second slip. The arrival of Adams, who joined Cottey in a snappy stand of 71, kept the momentum going, until the skipper clipped Younis powerfully off his pads only to be well caught by Ian Bell at square leg. Now in partnership with Tim Ambrose, about to keep wicket from the start for the first time in a Championship match since September 2001, Cottey, after tea, moved past 154, his previous best for Sussex, made at Chelmsford three years previously. The *cognoscenti,* complete with the *Playfair Cricket Annual*'s statistics, were ready to note the achievement and accordingly clapped. After nearly six hours' batting Cottey, who had hit 188 off 276 balls with 31 fours, succumbed to Alan Richardson, arguably the best of the eight bowlers Michael Powell tried. The same bowler then dismissed the impressive Ambrose, whose 50 had come off 104 balls, but with four points in the bag and one more in the offing Sussex, at 395 for five wickets, had had an excellent day against the Bears whom they had not beaten since 1991.

On the Saturday morning Waqar castled Robin Martin-Jenkins early in the piece, yorked Mark Davis and had Mushtaq caught. The overnight score of 395 for five had quickly become 439 for eight and Waqar's ten-over spell had three wickets for 28 runs. Help was on hand for Sussex, and Matthew Prior, all power and panache, joined a more studious James Kirtley in a stand worth 80 runs before Prior, having completed his 100 off 133 balls with 14 fours and a six, came unstuck against Brown just three balls later. It mattered little; on 545 all out Sussex were firmly in the driving seat.

James Kirtley bowls with an attacking field against Warwickshire at Hove at the end of June after the completion of the Twenty20 Cup programme.

Warwickshire suffered an early loss when Nick Knight, recently retired from international cricket, was adjudged lbw to Jason Lewry. Umpires tend to be hard on batsmen when they fail to offer a stroke, but from sideways-on in the pavilion it looked as if the ball might have gone over the top. Powell batted firmly to reach his 50 off 69 balls, but in the 16th over Adams decided to try Mushtaq, who immediately started to cause mayhem. Powell was so unsettled that he gloved Martin-Jenkins to the wicketkeeper and Wagh and Bell were totally bamboozled. The former, who had played the seamers confidently on a track which one correspondent described as 'smooth as a velveteen rug', edged to silly point, while Bell was in a rare pickle, hardly knowing whether to play back or come down the track and ending up almost on his knees as he was pinned lbw. When Kirtley had Jonathan Trott held in the gully and Obuya lbw and Mushtaq's throw had run out Frost, the Bears had collapsed to 140 for seven. Melvyn Betts chanced his arm before being caught at extra cover and, although Brown and Waqar held on until the close, Warwickshire on 194 for eight were still 202 off the follow-on target.

The pitch continued to play well on the Sunday morning, but it was the magic of Mushtaq that caused Warwickshire to fail to prolong the match into the fourth day. He quickly polished off their first innings and, when Adams enforced the follow-on, it seemed initially that they would make a fight of it, as Knight and Powell reached 116 without loss at lunchtime and eventually put on 135 for the 1st wicket. They had, it

Above Mushtaq bowls to Warwickshire captain Michael Powell with Ambrose, Adams, Goodwin and Montgomerie in close attendance.

Opposite Jason Lewry bowls against Warwickshire with umpire Vanburn Holder officiating.

seemed, coped reasonably well with Mushtaq, but then, with a selection of leg-spinners, googlies and flippers, the Pakistani magician, as vociferous as ever, set to work. With their concentration apparently ruined by what must have been an excellent lunch, Powell, Knight and Wagh fell to him in three consecutive overs, all caught close to the wicket and, although there was a lull in the debacle when Mushtaq was rested with leg cramps and Ian Bell batted two hours for 37, Mushtaq returned after tea as the batsmen went in and out again in rapid succession. His efforts were supported splendidly at the other end by the less penetrative, but far less histrionic off-spin of Mark Davis, whose two wickets were taken at a cost of little more than two runs per over. It seemed as if the pair, who had previously played only three four-day games together, would be seen more often in tandem and that Davis would receive more chances, probably at the expense of Kevin Innes, if the summer continued to be warm and dry.

Mushtaq's seven wickets gave him 11 for 140 in the match and this fifth five-wicket haul brought him to 52 wickets for the season. Having celebrated his thirty-third birthday on the Saturday, he must have relished the thought of the bonus he had earned by reaching his half-century of wickets, but the Sussex accountants may perhaps have taken a slightly different view.

Sussex (22 points) beat Warwickshire (3 points) by an innings and 59 runs.

Chris Adams leaps enthusiastically as Mushtaq bowls the last Warwickshire batsman, Alan Richardson, at Hove.

SUSSEX v WARWICKSHIRE

at Hove on 27th - 30th June - Frizzell County Championship Division 1

* Captain, + Wicket-Keeper

Sussex won the toss and elected to bat

SUSSEX — 1st Innings

#	Batsman	Dismissal	Runs
1	R.R. Montgomerie [7]	c: Frost b: Brown	66
2	M.W. Goodwin [3]	c: Frost b: Waqar	0
3	P.A. Cottey [2]	c: Frost b: Richardson	188
4	C.J. Adams * [1]	c: Bell b: Waqar	31
5	T.R. Ambrose + [11]	b: Richardson	50
6	R.S.C. Martin-Jenkins [12]	b: Waqar	28
7	M.J. Prior [13]	c: Frost b: Brown	100
8	M.J.G. Davis [8]	b: Waqar	6
9	Mushtaq Ahmed [9]	c: Trott b: Waqar	2
10	R.J. Kirtley [6]	not out	40
11	J.D. Lewry [5]	b: Brown	6
12	K.J. Innes [15]		

b 1	lb 9	wd 0	nb 18	Extras 28
Overs	147.1		Provisional Total	545
Pens	0	Wkts	10	Total 545

Fall of wickets — 1st Inns: 1 - 3 2 - 168 3 - 239 4 - 342 5 - 357 6 - 407 7 - 431 8 - 439 9 - 519 10 - 545

Bonus Points - Sussex 5, Warwks 2

Bowling

	Ovs	Md	R	Wk	wd	nb
Waqar Younis	24	2	99	5	0	1
Betts	20	1	91	0	0	4
Brown	31.1	8	95	3	0	1
Richardson	34	6	92	2	0	1
Bell	3	0	24	0	0	0
Obuya	19	1	89	0	0	2
Wagh	14	1	40	0	0	0
Trott	2	1	5	0	0	0

WARWKS

Following-on / 344 behind

#	Batsman		1st Innings	Runs		2nd Innings	Runs
1	N.V. Knight		Lbw b: Lewry	11		c: Prior b: Mushtaq	64
2	M.J. Powell *		c: Ambrose b: Martin-Jenkins	60		c: Adams b: Mushtaq	80
3	I.R. Bell	(4)	Lbw b: Mushtaq	0	(4)	c: Martin-Jenkins b: Mushtaq	37
4	M.A. Wagh	(3)	c: Prior b: Mushtaq	39	(3)	c: Prior b: Mushtaq	2
5	I.J.L. Trott		c: Goodwin b: Kirtley	6		Lbw b: Davis	31
6	D.R. Brown	(7)	not out	42	(7)	c: Adams b: Mushtaq	20
7	T. Frost +	(6)	Run Out (Mushtaq/Ambrose)	1	(6)	b: Davis	4
8	A. Richardson	(11)	b: Mushtaq	0	(11)	c: Ambrose b: Mushtaq	0
9	C.O. Obuya	(8)	Lbw b: Kirtley	2	(9)	not out	8
10	M.M. Betts	(9)	c: Davis b: Mushtaq	21		c: Adams b: Lewry	15
11	Waqar Younis	(10)	c: Ambrose b: Kirtley	8	(10)	c: Kirtley b: Mushtaq	14
12	N.M.K. Smith						

b 1	lb 9	wd 1	nb 0	Extras 11	b 2	lb 7	wd 1	nb 0	Extras 10
Overs	59.5		Provisional Total	201	Overs	92.4		Provisional Total	285
Pens	0	Wkts	10	Total 201	Pens	0	Wkts	10	Total 285

Fall of wickets — 1st Inns: 1 - 22 2 - 104 3 - 105 4 - 122 5 - 124 6 - 131 7 - 140 8 - 171 9 - 198 10 - 201

2nd Inns: 1 - 135 2 - 139 3 - 146 4 - 185 5 - 196 6 - 236 7 - 249 8 - 267 9 - 284 10 - 285

Bonus Points - Warwks 1, Sussex 3

Bowling

	Ovs	Md	R	Wk	wd	nb	Ovs	Md	R	Wk	wd	nb
Kirtley	15	2	57	3	1	0	16	2	62	0	1	0
Lewry	10	2	35	1	0	0	9	2	41	1	0	0
Mushtaq Ahmed	22.5	6	55	4	0	0	32.4	9	85	7	0	0
Martin-Jenkins	10	1	40	1	0	0	12	4	38	0	0	0
Davis	2	1	4	0	0	0	23	6	50	2	0	0

SUSSEX WON BY AN INNINGS AND 59 RUNS

UMPIRES :
M.J. Kitchen
V. Holder

SCORERS :
J.F. Hartridge
D.E. Wainwright

HOURS OF PLAY
Days 1 - 3: 11am - 6.30pm
Day 4 : 11am - 6pm

Lunch
Days 1 - 3: 1.15pm - 1.55pm
Day 4 : 1pm - 1.40pm

Tea
Days 1 - 3 : 4.10pm - 4.30pm
or when 32 overs remain to
be bowled, whichever is later
Day 4 : 3.40pm - 4pm

1st Inns Bonus Pts
(Only in the first 130 Overs)

Batting (Max 5pts)
1pt at achieving 200, 250,
300, 350 and 400 runs.

Bowling (Max 3pts)
1 pt for taking 3, 6 & 9 wkts

SUSSEX v. ESSEX AT ARUNDEL CASTLE

Wednesday to Saturday, 9 to 12 July 2003

With the demise of Worthing and Chichester's Priory Park as first-class cricket grounds Sussex have brought cricket to the western side of the county by playing at Arundel. The first Championship match took place in 1990 and since that time county matches have been played on this remarkably beautiful ground with Arundel Castle peeping through the trees at the cricketers. The facilities may not match those of many a county headquarters – the pavilion, for instance, is more what one might expect of a club-cricket ground – but for sheer arboreal beauty you can't beat Arundel.

On a gloriously warm and sunny morning in front of a good crowd Ronnie Irani must have been pleased to win the toss and consign Sussex to a day in the field. The ever-reliable James Kirtley, however, soon struck and, with the fifth ball of his first over, he sent an out-of-form Paul Grayson back across the field and up the many steps to the pavilion. James Foster, nowadays out of favour with England's selectors despite some gritty performances, was in quite high at number 3 and was soon undone by Jason Lewry's extra bounce, a juggling Richard Montgomerie holding him at first slip. At 23 for two wickets Essex were not making the most of their chances, but England Test captain Nasser Hussain and former Zimbabwe skipper Andy Flower set about repairing the damage with a useful partnership of 72, before umpire David Constant decided that a second Kirtley appeal against Flower was worth upholding. It seemed as if the batsman took a different view, suggesting that the ball might have gone over the top of the stumps. In the 13th over Chris Adams brought on Mushtaq from the Park End and allowed the pacemen to enjoy the extra bounce from the Castle End.

Lewry was probably the pick of the Sussex seamers, and he added Aftab Habib and skipper Irani fairly quickly to his victims during the afternoon, while a classic battle between Hussain and Mushtaq continued. It has often been suggested that the county game offers little of the tension and cut-and-thrust required for the Test arena, but this was undoubtedly a high-class contest. Hussain, born in Madras, and Mushtaq, born a mere 1,500 miles away in Sahiwal, battled it out and the England captain looked to dominate Mushtaq in a way in which no other batsman, except perhaps Graham Thorpe, had achieved in the 2003 season. Who won? Probably Hussain, but only just. In the end Mushtaq had him taken at silly mid-off where Montgomerie made an excellent reflex catch, but the little wizard had by the close – by which time Graham Napier had scored a Championship best – taken just the one wicket for 102 runs. At 305 with eight wickets down, Essex might have felt that they missed a chance to compile a really massive total, but Napier and Ryan ten Doeschate, having added 90 together, were still there and ready for the next morning.

The Thursday morning enjoyed just the same glorious weather as that of the first day and Napier batted well for his 89 and Essex closed on 340, probably at least 60 below what they might have achieved, while Lewry basked in his first five-wicket haul of the season. Sussex, in reply, made a poor start as Zimbabwe-born left-arm pace-bowler Scott Brant had Goodwin and Montgomerie back in the pavilion with only 13 on the board. Adams came in and looked ready to take the attack to Essex, but when he had made 20 crisp runs he was caught behind. It is sad that he often edges the ball to be

Tim Ambrose pushes forward defensively against Essex against the backdrop of the pavilion at the beautiful Arundel Castle ground at the beginning of July.

taken behind the wicket or in the slips when he is starting to make batting look a different ball game from any other batsman. At 53 for three wickets Sussex needed to be dug out of a hole if they were to maintain their recent form. Fortunately they had in their service Tony Cottey and Tim Ambrose, two of the shorter members of the batting fraternity, but also players who are incredibly quick on their feet. They added 178 together before Ambrose was brilliantly caught at slip off Grayson's slow left-arm spinners and, just to prove the old saying that one wicket brings two, Cottey immediately hooked Dakin carelessly to deep square leg to end a 211-ball innings which contained ten fours and a six. Grayson, who had not had much success with the ball in the season to date, now removed Robin Martin-Jenkins and Mark Davis, while Brant sent back Prior. Having reduced Sussex to 282 for eight wickets by the close, Essex must have felt that they had just got their noses in front.

Essex failed to build on their slight advantage of the evening before when the match continued on the Friday morning. The Sussex bowling trio of Mushtaq, Kirtley and Lewry all made useful scores and Sussex finally gained a modest lead of 19. The batting surface had now become slower and Essex, in their second innings, started to grind out a respectable total that might conceivably win them the match, especially as Sussex had to bat last. Hussain was caught by Mushtaq off a steepling hit at long leg and Foster was

Left James Kirtley receives the Frizzell County Championship award for the month of May in the course of the Essex match at Arundel.

Opposite Tim Ambrose congratulates Tony Cottey on reaching his hundred against Essex.

run out by a smart return from Lewry, but Grayson, Flower and Habib all made competent half-centuries and, closing on 254 for six wickets off 82 overs, they seemed to have taken the initiative away from Sussex. Mushtaq bowled 24 wicketless overs for 87 runs and only the steadiness of Lewry and Mark Davis's off-spin had kept their side in the game.

It was the turn of Essex to squander their chances on the Saturday morning, as Lewry blew away their tail for a total of 274 and completed a ten-wicket match haul. This left Sussex to score 256 from a minimum of 82 overs. Once again the openers and Adams failed and Sussex were placed precariously on 53 for three. Three of Sussex's top four had at this stage in the season contributed just one century and six fifties between them in the Championship and it had been left to Cottey and the middle order to rescue the side. This day was no different. Cottey and Ambrose looked as if they were continuing where they had left off in the first innings, adding on this occasion 172 for the 4th wicket off 56 overs before Cottey, who had faced 183 balls and hit eight fours, edged a catch behind off Dakin when two short of what would have been his third consecutive ton. It was certainly a purple patch for him and meant that he had passed 50 in six of his last seven innings. At 204 for four Sussex were now virtually home and dry, and Ambrose and Martin-Jenkins knocked off the last 53 runs with 4.5 overs to spare. Ambrose just

failed to reach what would have been a thoroughly well-deserved ton, his 93 not out coming off 214 balls with 11 fours.

The after-match comments touched on a number of issues. Ambrose was full of praise for 'Cotts', saying, 'I have learned such a lot from the two times I have batted with him this week and, as far as I'm concerned, he's a legend.' Peter Moores was equally happy with Cottey's form, being quoted in *The Sunday Telegraph* as saying: 'Performance is king in this game and Tony Cottey is at the stage of his career where, if he is playing well, then he may want to continue his cricket career. What is certain is that he is playing beautifully at the moment, probably better than he has played for many years.' It must have been what a thirty-seven-year-old wanted to hear when he was in the last year of his five-year contract.

Chris Adams, Sussex's skipper, was more cautious after the game than one might have expected as Sussex moved into second place in the table. 'We're on a journey towards winning the Championship,' he told *The Argus* at the end of the match, 'and even if it doesn't happen this year, then I'm convinced our time will come.'

Sussex (21 points) beat Essex (6 points) by six wickets.

SUSSEX v ESSEX

at Arundel on 9th - 12th July - Frizzell County Championship Division 1

Essex won the toss and elected to bat

* Captain, + Wicket-Keeper

MATCH SPONSOR - P@v - i.t. services

SUSSEX		1st Innings	R	2nd Innings	R
1	R.R. Montgomerie [7]	c: Hussain b: Brant	1	c: Foster b: Dakin	1
2	M.W. Goodwin [3]	b: Brant	11	b: Dakin	18
3	P.A. Cottey [2]	c: Middlebrook b: Dakin	107	c: Foster b: Dakin	98
4	C.J. Adams * [1]	c: Foster b: Napier	20	c: Habib b: Middlebrook	0
5	T.R. Ambrose + [11]	c: Flower b: Grayson	88	not out	93
6	R.S.C. Martin-Jenkins [12]	Lbw b: Grayson	6	not out	21
7	M.J. Prior [13]	Lbw b: Brant	13		
8	M.J.G. Davis [8]	c: Habib b: Grayson	12		
9	Mushtaq Ahmed [9]	c: Dakin b: Grayson	34		
10	R.J. Kirtley [6]	not out	35		
11	J.D. Lewry [5]	c: Flower b: Middlebrook	22		
12	K.J. Innes [15]				

				Extras						Extras	
b 0	lb 3	wd 3	nb 4	10	b 7	lb 4	wd 15	nb 0		26	
Overs	110.5	Provisional Total	359		Overs	77.1	Provisional Total	257			
Pens	0	Wkts	10	Total	359	Pens	0	Wkts	4	Total	257

Fall of wickets
1st Inns: 1-4, 2-13, 3-53, 4-231, 5-233, 6-250, 7-254, 8-280, 9-323, 10-359
2nd Inns: 1-1, 2-31, 3-32, 4-204

Bonus Points - Sussex 4, Essex 3

Bowling	Ovs	Md	R	Wk	wd	nb	Ovs	Md	R	Wk	wd	nb
Dakin	25	5	67	1	0	0	16	2	54	3	0	0
Brant	25	4	90	3	2	0	7	0	27	0	1	0
ten Doeschate	10	3	53	0	0	2	-	-	-	-	-	-
Napier	16	2	45	1	0	0	7	0	24	0	0	0
Middlebrook	17.5	3	54	1	0	0	23.1	1	78	1	0	0
Grayson	17	2	47	4	3	0	24	7	63	0	9	0

ESSEX		1st Innings	R	2nd Innings	R
1	A.P. Grayson	c: Grayson b: Kirtley	0	b: Davis	71
2	N. Hussain	c: Montgomerie b: Mushtaq	95	c: Mushtaq b: Lewry	22
3	J.S. Foster +	c: Montgomerie b: Lewry	12	Run Out	1
4	A. Flower	Lbw b: Kirtley	37	Lbw b: Davis	54
5	A. Habib	c: Ambrose b: Lewry	0	c: Ambrose b: Lewry	53
6	R.C. Irani *	c: Adams b: Lewry	15	c: Adams b: Davis	6
7	J.D. Middlebrook	Lbw b: Martin-Jenkins	14	c: Adams b: Lewry	23
8	J.M. Dakin	c: Kirtley b: Lewry	12	(9) b: Lewry	0
9	G.R. Napier	not out	89	(10) not out	10
10	R.N. ten Doeschate	b: Lewry	31	(8) Lbw b: Mushtaq	6
11	S. Brant	c: Prior b: Mushtaq	3	b: Lewry	2
12					

				Extras						Extras	
b 2	lb 7	wd 0	nb 0	9	b 0	lb 19	wd 5	nb 2		26	
Overs	114.5	Provisional Total	340		Overs	93.4	Provisional Total	274			
Pens	0	Wkts	10	Total	340	Pens	0	Wkts	10	Total	274

Fall of wickets
1st Inns: 1-0, 2-23, 3-95, 4-97, 5-115, 6-149, 7-203, 8-215, 9-331, 10-340
2nd Inns: 1-49, 2-50, 3-140, 4-187, 5-193, 6-243, 7-258, 8-262, 9-262, 10-274

Bonus Points - Essex 3, Sussex 3

Bowling	Ovs	Md	R	Wk	wd	nb	Ovs	Md	R	Wk	wd	nb
Kirtley	24	4	88	2	0	0	17	2	48	0	1	1
Lewry	29	7	72	5	0	0	19.4	6	52	5	0	0
Mushtaq Ahmed	36.5	10	102	2	0	0	30	4	92	1	0	0
Martin-Jenkins	17	3	44	1	0	0	8	3	19	0	0	0
Davis	8	0	25	0	0	0	19	3	44	3	0	0

SUSSEX WON BY 6 WICKETS

UMPIRES :
B. Leadbeater
D.J. Constant
SCORERS :
J.F. Hartridge
D. Norris
HOURS OF PLAY
Days 1 - 3 : 11am - 6.30pm
Day 4 : 11am - 6pm
Lunch
Days 1 - 3 : 1.15pm - 1.55pm
Day 4 : 1pm - 1.40pm
Tea
Days 1 - 3 : 4.10pm - 4.30pm
or when 32 overs remain to be bowled, whichever is later
Day 4 : 3.40pm - 4pm
1st Inns Bonus Pts
(Only in the first 130 Overs)
Batting (Max 5pts)
1pt at achieving 200, 250, 300, 350 and 400 runs.
Bowling (Max 3pts)
1 pt for taking 3, 6 & 9 wkts

Opposite Jason Lewry runs in to bowl past umpire Barrie Leadbeater in the county's match with Essex at Arundel.

SUSSEX v. LEICESTERSHIRE AT LEICESTER

Tuesday to Friday, 15 to 18 July 2003

Sussex were pulled up sharp at Grace Road by Leicestershire's captain Phillip DeFreitas who, after winning the toss and deciding to bat, saw his side collapse before he himself scored a boisterous hundred which put a vastly different complexion on matters. The home side were without the injured Indian overseas player Virender Sehwag, and a new opening combination of John Maunders, signed from Middlesex, and Darren Stevens failed to get underway. Maunders survived an lbw appeal from James Kirtley's first ball of the day, but was less successful second ball. Stevens and Darren Maddy added 60 before Mushtaq appeared on the scene. Maddy missed a straight one and was lbw, and at 107 Stevens overbalanced and was smartly stumped by Tim Ambrose. Mushtaq quickly disposed of Trevor Ward and Paul Nixon, and then Brad Hodge, the hosts' accomplished Australian, was snapped up for 47 off bat and pad by Richard Montgomerie at short leg. Mushtaq's wiles, to say nothing of his vocal chords, had accounted for five of the first six batsmen and Leicestershire were staring down the barrel at 154 for six.

DeFreitas, who had begun his first-class career at Grace Road in 1985, must be keen on his English geography, for he played his cricket at Old Trafford between 1989 and 1993 and then sampled the Derbyshire scenery for six seasons between 1994 and 1999, only to return home in 2000. Appointed to the captaincy in 2003, he doubtless wished to show that his decision to bat first on a slow and easy-paced pitch was a wise one. Sadly, his batsmen had not agreed and he had to take charge himself. Batting with the obdurate Jeremy Snape, he advanced the total to 250 for seven and then added a further 69 with number 10 Charlie Dagnall, so that when he had completed the 10th century of his career off 116 balls, he must have felt that the task was completed with his side on 320. Mushtaq had continued to whirl away in a forlorn hope for a sixth wicket, and Kevin Innes and Robin Martin-Jenkins had both come in for some stick from the Leicester skipper.

Sussex's openers, Goodwin and Montgomerie, who had competently moved to 50 overnight, would surely have realised that on the flat Leicester track a significant total was within the side's grasp. It was DeFreitas who also took the lead on the bowling front and captured the first three Sussex wickets. He brought one back sharply to trap Goodwin lbw in the first session, but there then followed a century partnership between Tony Cottey and Montgomerie. The former gave his partner an 18-over start and still beat him to 50 and, after 103 had been added, DeFreitas bowled Montgomerie after a dour innings of 176 balls. He then inflicted on Adams his fourth duck of the season, trapping him lbw second ball. Worse was to follow: Ambrose had his leg stump uprooted by Dagnall, who also trapped Martin-Jenkins lbw with one that kept unsportingly low.

At 215 for five Sussex were facing a crisis, but the 5ft 4ins Cottey was not flustered and his lack of height may have allowed him to deal well with balls of low bounce, while at the same time he was not slow to advance down the wicket on nimble feet or pull through the leg side. Now joined by Prior, who played the most fluent innings of the day, he was able to guide Sussex through to 340 for five at the close. His value to

Tony Cottey sweeps on his way to 147 against Leicestershire at Grace Road in the middle of July.

the County was put into perspective when it was seen that this was his third century of the season, while his colleagues have made only four between them. On the Thursday morning Sussex did not really capitalise on their previous success: Cottey added only ten to his overnight 137 before being taken at the wicket off the consistent DeFreitas and, although Prior batted on to four short of his hundred, the last five wickets fell for 46 runs and a fifth batting point eluded them as the score after 130 overs was only 388 for seven. This may have been due, in part at least, to the DeFreitas policy of containment, employing few close fielders and allowing his seam bowlers to bowl line and length on an unresponsive pitch.

Rain had been predicted for the Thursday, but the weather gods smiled on Sussex and only the last hour of the day was lost, by which time Mushtaq, aided by Kirtley and Innes had made inroads into the Leicestershire second innings. Maunders and Stevens, who put on 70 for the 1st wicket, were both pinned lbw on the back foot by Mushtaq, as was Nixon some time later. Kirtley accounted for the dangerous Hodge and Innes dismissed Maddy off a top-edged pull. At the close, with the home side on 186 for five, they were 90 runs on and Sussex could sniff victory as long as the weather played fair.

On the final morning Trevor Ward and Snape continued to offer sound resistance and the score reached 225 for five when Ward was adjudged caught off bat and pad at silly point. These sorts of dismissals are always fraught, particularly when the Mushtaq appeal is so cacophonous, and Ward was sure there was more pad and no bat in his shot, but his dismissal turned the innings. The last five wickets fell for the addition of 33 runs, which left Sussex to score 163 to win. Mushtaq, taking ten for 189 off almost 75 overs – ten wickets in a match for the third time in the season – showed considerable endurance and he was always going to be a handful against one of the weaker batting outfits in Division One.

Sussex made hard work of scoring the runs they needed to clinch their sixth win of the season and their fourth in succession at Grace Road, as Goodwin chopped on, Montgomerie was bowled trying to pull to square leg and Adams trapped in front for the second time in the match. These three wickets were down before 100 was on the board, but the reliable Cottey was on hand to notch another half-century with eight fours and a six, enjoying a stand of 62 in 12 overs with Ambrose after tea. By 4.45 p.m., however, it was all over, and Surrey's lead at the top of the Championship had been cut to just five points. Skipper Chris Adams, as ever, remained guarded. 'Surrey,' he said after the match, 'remain the strongest outfit in the league.' The match at Hove with Surrey at the end of July was obviously going to be a showdown.

Sussex (21 points) beat Leicestershire (5 points) by five wickets.

LEICESTERSHIRE v SUSSEX

Frizzell County Championship
15, 16, 17, 18 July, 2003
Grace Road, Leicester

Toss won by Leicestershire who elected to bat
UMPIRES: P.J. Hartley and J.F.Steele
SCORERS: G.A.York and J.F.Hartridge

*captain #wicket-keeper

Matchday Hosts
Humberts

LEICESTERSHIRE

Batsman	First innings		Second innings	
J.K.Maunders	lbw b Kirtley	0	lbw b Mushtaq	27
D.I.Stevens	st Ambrose b Mushtaq	51	lbw b Mushtaq	50
D.L.Maddy	lbw b Mushtaq	30	cM-Jenkins b Innes	40
B.J.Hodge	cMontgomerie bMushtaq	47	lbw b Kirtley	18
T.R.Ward	lbw b Mushtaq	4	c Prior b Mushtaq	50
#P.A.Nixon	b Mushtaq	4	lbw b Mushtaq	11
J.N.Snape	b Kirtley	36	run out	20
*P.A. DeFreitas	b Martin-Jenkins	103	c Goodwin b M-Jenkins	8
D.D.Masters	run out	0	c Ambrose b M-Jenkins	0
C.E.Dagnall	not out	15	c Cottey b Mushtaq	15
R.M.Amin	b Martin-Jenkins	0	not out	6
Extras	(b1, lb22, w5, nb2)	30	(b1, lb9, w3)	13
TOTAL	(85.5 overs)	320	(95.5 overs)	258

1/0,2/60,3/107,4/123,5/127,6/154,7/250,8/251,9/320 f0/320

1/70,2/93,3/128,4/150,5/162,6/225 7/234,8/234,9/237,10/258

BOWLING

	O	M	R	W		O	M	R	W
Kirtley	21	6	68	2		22	7	72	1
Lewry	6	1	18	0		-			
Martin-Jenkins	13.5	1	66	2		25	9	53	2
Mushtaq	33	4	93	5		41.5	18	96	5
Innes	12	1	52	0		7	1	27	1

SUSSEX

Batsman	First innings		Second innings	
M.W.Goodwin	lbw b DeFreitas	34	b Masters	11
R.Montgomerie	b DeFreitas	52	b Amin	28
P.A.Cottey	c Nixon bDeFreitas	147	b Amin	58
*C.J.Adams	lbw b DeFreitas	0	lbw b Maddy	16
#T.R.Ambrose	b Dagnall	2	b Snape	25
R. M-Jenkins	lbw b Dagnall	7	not out	6
M.J.Prior	c Hodge b Maddy	96	not out	4
K.J.Innes	not out	14		
Mushtaq Ahmed	st Nixon b Amin	21		
R.J.Kirtley	c Maunders b Amin	0		
J.D.Lewry	c Snape bDeFreitas	0		
Extras	(b15, lb16, w2, nb10)	43	(b10, lb2, w2, nb4)	18
TOTAL	(137.5 overs)	416	(38.5 overs; 5 wkts)	166

1/58,2/161,3/161,4/187,5/215,6/370,7/382,8/415, 9/415,10/416

1/30,2/48,3/96,4/156,5/158

BOWLING

	O	M	R	W		O	M	R	W
Dagnall	30	10	87	2		2	0	20	0
Masters	27	5	89	2		8.2	1	31	1
Amin	19	5	50	2		11	1	41	2
Maddy	17	1	70	1		7	0	23	1
Snape	4	0	10	0		1.5	0	6	1
DeFreitas	29.5	10	55	5		2.4	0	5	0
Maunders	5	0	12	0		-			
Stevens	5	1	11	0		-			
Hodge	1	0	1	0		6	0	28	0

SUSSEX WON BY 5 WICKETS

SUSSEX *v.* NOTTINGHAMSHIRE AT TRENT BRIDGE
Friday to Monday, 25 to 28 July 2003

If they were going to take the lead at the top of the County Championship Sussex needed to beat Nottinghamshire at Trent Bridge and make it a double after their convincing win at Horsham in late May, but they were not helped in their bid by the rain which washed out the whole of Friday, the first day of the match.

Play was possible on the Saturday morning and, after Chris Adams had won the toss, Murray Goodwin and Richard Montgomerie set off to give their side a good start. Two seasons ago, when Sussex became Division Two Champions, the pair had formed the most prolific opening partnership in county cricket, scoring 2,982 Championship runs with 13 hundreds and nine fifties between them. In the current season the well seemed to be running dry and Goodwin, a Test batsman and good enough to get into the Western Australia side in the winter, had managed a mere 496 runs from 17 Championship innings before this match, while Montgomerie had also failed to score consistently. The batting success which Sussex had up until then enjoyed had been due to the performances of Tony Cottey and the middle order – players such as Tim Ambrose and Matt Prior, not to mention Robin Martin-Jenkins.

In the opening half-hour it was easy to see why the openers had not been scoring the expected runs. The ball was swinging and there was some life in the Trent Bridge pitch and the Nottinghamshire bowlers ought to have made life difficult for Sussex. In fact, they had problems in maintaining with any consistency a line that would test the batsmen. Andrew Harris was bowling wide of the off stump and swinging it away further, thus allowing the batsmen to shoulder arms to over 50 per cent of the balls in his first spell, while Charlie Shreck, rather more penetrative, caused some false shots to be played, but failed to take a wicket. In the end New Zealander Chris Cairns came on as first change and dismissed Montgomerie for 32 with a ball that pitched just short and seamed away to take the edge. Sussex were left still awaiting their first century opening partnership of the season, but this was the hosts' only success before lunch. Cairns, although finding movement off the seam, bowled a fair number of 'four balls' which Goodwin and Tony Cottey put away with ease.

After lunch the pattern was repeated. Although Cairns beat Goodwin with two 'jaffas' in one over, he also conceded two boundaries at the same time, and it was left to Shreck to hold the scoring down. He too occasionally dropped short and Cottey pulled him to the mid-wicket boundary to reach his ninth half-century in ten Championship innings. Taking a liberty too many, Cottey cut Franks to deep third man, after which Goodwin soon reached his hundred, his first of the season, which had taken only 167 balls. Goodwin was joined by Adams, and together they plundered 98 runs from only 16 overs, taking a particular fancy to the off-spin of Kevin Pietersen, who was struck for a straight six by Adams and for a six and two fours off successive balls by his partner. With the score on 295 Adams was caught at long leg and, two runs later, Goodwin played down the wrong line and was bowled for an excellent 148. It seemed as if, after his lean

Opposite Robin Martin-Jenkins reached the third century of his career against Nottinghamshire at Trent Bridge at the end of July.

spell, he was running into form at a critical time in Sussex's bid for the Championship. When a further wasted hour was added to the loss of the whole of the previous day's play, Sussex must have felt, as a circumspect Michael Yardy and a more ebullient Martin-Jenkins took them to 355 scored at a rate of nearly four runs an over, that they had made the best of the chances offered to them.

Sussex needed to push on quickly on the Sunday morning and Martin-Jenkins, in completing a robust first century of the season off 128 balls, together with Yardy, Prior and Innes, saw to it that 142 runs were added in 21.4 overs, allowing a declaration to come before the end of the fourth session. Sussex had given themselves approximately 175 overs to bowl Nottinghamshire out twice.

Needing 348 to avoid the follow-on, the home side started disastrously, losing three wickets for 46, all to James Kirtley, whose first spell was three for 15. Subsequently, Pietersen, who hopes to play Test cricket for England, took charge, first with Russell Warren and then, after the fall of two quick wickets, with Paul Franks so that his side ended the day on 289 for seven wickets, still needing 59 to save the follow-on.

To take 13 wickets on the final day proved a task too demanding for Sussex. After a smart catch by Adams at first slip off Kirtley had ended Pietersen's fine innings, Nottinghamshire soon collapsed, leaving them 201 in arrears and required to follow-on with 87 overs remaining. Kirtley, who had taken a well-deserved 'five-for' in the first innings, trapped Jason Gallian lbw with the fourth ball of the second and Paul Hutchison removed Guy Welton. A 3rd-wicket stand of 110 between Darren Bicknell and Warren in 27 overs, however, proved a stumbling block for Sussex and put the home side on the path to saving the match. Montgomerie and Prior came close to catching Bicknell when he was on 26 and 30, but the pitch was now slow and unresponsive and Warren went on to a chanceless maiden hundred for Nottinghamshire, adding 131 with Pietersen who came close to scoring a second hundred in the match. The trump card of Mushtaq had been nullified by the pitch and, finally, Sussex allowed Cottey and Montgomerie to bowl the closing overs as the latter succeeded in taking the second first-class wicket of his career.

After the match Peter Moores, talking to *The Argus* was upbeat about the County's further chances. 'It all went well until the Bicknell-Warren partnership,' he said, 'but I'm happy with a 12-point draw, particularly away from home. It leaves us tucked in behind Surrey and it's not a bad position to be in, bearing in mind the amount of points left to play for. Mushtaq, of course, wasn't as effective as we would have liked because the pitch was so slow, but the seamers gave it everything.'

Sussex (12 points) drew with Nottinghamshire (8 points).

NOTTINGHAMSHIRE

	1st innings		2nd innings	
1. J E R GALLIAN (1)*	b. Kirtley	6	lbw b. Kirtley	0
2. G E WELTON (19)	c. Yardy b. Kirtley	12	c. Cottey b. Hutchison	8
3. D J BICKNELL (2)	c. Prior+ b. Kirtley	15	c. Mont'rie b. Kirtley	75
4. R J WARREN (16)	c. Cottey b. M-Jenkins	42	Not Out	114
5. K P PIETERSEN (6)	c. Adams b. Kirtley	139	c. and b. Mont'rie	81
6. C L CAIRNS (5)	c. Prior+ b. M-Jenkins	1	Not Out	7
7. C M W READ (7)+	c.Mont'rie b. Ahmed	0	Did Not Bat	
8. P J FRANKS (8)	c. Yardy b. Hutchison	43	Did Not Bat	
9. G D CLOUGH (15)	c. Adams b. Ahmed	16	Did Not Bat	
10. A J HARRIS (13)	b. Kirtley	1	Did Not Bat	
11. C E SHRECK (25)	Not Out	0	Did Not Bat	
	Extras	21	Extras	6
	TOTAL	296	TOTAL	291
	87.5 overs	All Out	For 4 Wkts DECLARED	
			INNINGS COMPLETED	

TOSS WON BY: SUSSEX who elected TO BAT
BONUS POINTS: 4

FALL OF WICKETS:
1- 16 2- 35 3- 46 4-127 5-139 6-140 7-254 8-290 9-296 10-296
1- 1 2- 34 3- 144 4-275 5- 6- 7- 8- 9- 10-

BOWLING ANALYSIS	O	M	R	WK	NB		O	M	R	WK	NB
R J KIRTLEY	23	9	60	5	3		11	4	32	2	-
P M HUTCHISON	17	5	60	1	-		16	2	66	1	-
MUSHTAQ AHMED	28.5	2	87	2	-		9	2	41	-	-
M H YARDY	5	-	14	-	-		13	2	50	-	-
R S C MARTIN-JENKINS	14	1	60	2	-		12	2	43	-	-
D A COTTEY	-	-	-	-	-		9	1	44	1	-
R R MONTGOMERIE	-	-	-	-	-		3	-	9	1	-

RESULT: MATCH DRAWN

SUSSEX

	1st innings		2nd innings	
1. R R MONTGOMERIE (7)	c. Read+ b. Cairns	32		10-
2. M W GOODWIN (3)	b. Clough	148		10-
3. P A COTTEY (2)	c. Harris b. Franks	53		
4. C J ADAMS (1)*	c. Franks b. Harris	46		
5. R S C MARTIN-JENKINS(12)	Not Out	121		
6. M H YARDY (-)	c. Read+ b. Harris	47		
7. M J PRIOR (13)+	c. Clough b. Franks	17		
8. MUSHTAQ AHMED (8)	Did Not Bat	-		
9. P M HUTCHISON (23)	Did Not Bat	-		
10. K J INNES (15)	Not Out	6		
11. R J KIRTLEY (-)	Did Not Bat	-		
	Extras	27	Extras	
	TOTAL	497	TOTAL	
	For 6 Wkts DECLARED			
	INNINGS COMPLETED			

BONUS POINTS: 7

FALL OF WICKETS:
1- 60 2- 197 3- 295 4- 297 5- 434 6-474 7- 8- 9- 10-

BOWLING ANALYSIS	O	M	R	WK	NB		O	M	R	WK	NB
A J HARRIS	28	5	98	2	1						
C E SHRECK	28	4	109	-	-						
C L CAIRNS	18	5	63	1	5						
P J FRANKS	19	3	102	2	4						
G D CLOUGH	16	-	76	1	-						
K P PIETERSEN	4	-	43	-	-						

PLAYER INFORMATION: * DENOTES COUNTY CAP

*R R MONTGOMERIE b Rugby, Warwicks 3 Jul 1971, RHB, OB, Deb 1999
*M W GOODWIN b Salisbury, Rhodesia 11 Dec 1972, RHB, LB, Deb 2001
*P A COTTEY b Swansea, Glamorgan, 2 Jun 1966, RHB, OB, Deb 1999
*C J ADAMS b Whitwell, Derbyshire 6 May 1970, RHB, RM/OB, Deb 1998
*R S C MARTIN-JENKINS b Guildford, Surrey 28 Oct 1975, RHB, RFM, Deb 1995
M H YARDY b Pembury, Kent 27 Nov 1980, LHB, LM, Deb 2000
M J PRIOR b Johannesburg, SA 24 Feb 1982, RHB, WK, Deb 2001
MUSHTAQ AHMED b Sahiwal, Pakistan 28 Jan 1970, RHB, LBG, Deb 2002
P M HUTCHISON b Leeds, Yorks 9 Jan 1977, LHB, LFM, Deb 2002
K J INNES b Wellingborough 24 Sep 1975, RHB, RM, Deb 2002
*R J KIRTLEY b Eastbourne 10 Jan 1975, RHB, RFM Deb 1995

*CAPTAIN +WICKETKEEPER
Notts players' squad numbers appear above in brackets after their names.
HOURS OF PLAY: Start 11.00am; Lunch (1st 3 days) 1.15-1.55pm; (4th day) 1.00-1.40pm;
Tea (1st 3 days) 4.10pm, provided that 32 overs or less remain to be bowled, (4th day) 3.40pm;
Close (1st 3 days) 6.30pm or 104 overs, (4th day) 6.00 pm or 96 overs.
POINTS FOR FRIZZELL COUNTY CHAMPIONSHIP MATCHES: 1st innings (1st 130 overs only)
BATTING 200 runs, 1 pt; 250 runs, 2pts; 300 runs, 3 pts; 350 runs, 4 pts; 400 runs, 5 pts;
BOWLING 3 wkts, 1 pt; 6 wkts, 2 pts; 9 wkts, 3 pts.
In addition: 14 pts for a win, 4 pts for a draw, 7 pts to the side batting fourth if the scores are level
PREVIOUS RESULTS v SUSSEX: First first-class match 1835.
Notts won 79, Sussex won 44, drawn 76. Home: Notts won 42, lost 17, drawn 40.
HS for Notts: 726 (1895); for Sussex 619-7d (2003). LS for Notts 57 (1962); for Sussex 19 (1873)
Individual Highest: Notts 268* J. A. Dixon (1897); Sussex 233 C. B. Fry (1905)
Best Bowling: Notts 9-23 Wm. Attewell (1886); Sussex: 8-23 A. Buss (1966)
Forthcoming matches: **30th, 31st, 1st & 2nd August 2003.** Notts v Middlesex at Trent Bridge, FCC. **3rd August 2003.** Notts v Lancashire Lightning at Cleethorpes, NCL.

SUSSEX v. SURREY AT HOVE
Wednesday to Saturday, 30 July to 2 August 2003

This match between the two leaders in the Championship was seen, for obvious reasons, as a crunch match, although finally it turned out to be rather less than that. One correspondent noted that Adam Hollioake had surely to know how Nasser Hussain felt – lose the toss in a vital game, watch your bowlers underperform and end the day wondering why, after a period when most things had gone right, it didn't just pan out correctly.

Just to rub salt into the Surrey wounds of losing the toss on a superb pitch, Sussex openers Richard Montgomerie and Murray Goodwin posted their first century stand of the season. After a year when the top order had prospered less than those lower down, the previous match at Trent Bridge had indicated that the opening pair were perhaps running into form at the right moment. They were certainly helped too by Martin Bicknell obviously feeling below par and by Jimmy Ormond consistently bowling too short. Goodwin cut and pulled as of yore and Montgomerie, apart from a few streaky shots through the slip cordon, suffered little by comparison. It took a good ball to break them up, but Ormond's first ball after lunch started to swing in and then cut away off the pitch to remove Goodwin's off stump.

One over before lunch Hollioake had introduced Saqlain into the attack at the Sea End and he bowled a marathon spell of 36 overs from there until the close. His only reward came fairly early when Tony Cottey, Sussex's recent hero with 651 runs to his credit in his previous four matches, went back instead of forward and was lbw. After that Chris Adams and Montgomerie added 82 before the latter, coming in sight of his second ton of the season, failed to pick Ian Salisbury's googly after he had spent 265 minutes at the crease. Salisbury must sometimes have pondered whether he had made the right move in 1997 by moving from Hove to The Oval; true, he was with a Championship-winning side and his Test prospects, together with his salary, were probably enhanced, but notwithstanding that he was also the second spinner to Saqlain. At Hove he would have been king until Mushtaq's arrival at the seaside.

Tim Ambrose joined Adams and together they added a further 98 before the keeper edged to slip for 43. Before the close, however, Adams came to his hundred, his first in the Championship since May 2002. He had batted for 229 minutes and faced 169 balls, so when he raised his bat in acknowledgement it may have been more with relief than with elation. By reaching 362 for four and taking four batting points, while Surrey were labouring for just one bowling point, Sussex must have felt that they had taken the first round.

The success which Adams had enjoyed on the first day was soon dissipated when he gloved the second ball of the day down the leg side to be caught brilliantly by 'keeper Jonathan Batty, who dived far to his left. Neither bowler nor keeper appealed and umpire Mark Benson shook his head, but Adams, sportingly, made his own decision and walked off. It was reassuring, in these confrontational and occasionally dishonest days, to see the spirit of cricket upheld, but the fact of the matter was that a splendid overnight score became transformed into 429 all out – a sound performance against a good team, but certainly disappointing in the context. Ormond had pitched the ball much further up than he had done on the previous day and his swing accounted for Matt Prior and

Richard Montgomerie bats against Saqlain
Mushtaq on his way to 90 in the crunch
match with Surrey at Hove at the end of
July and the beginning of August.

Mark Davis who were both caught in the slips. In fact, a fifth batting point looked in
doubt until Robin Martin-Jenkins and Mushtaq added 48 for the 8th wicket, the latter
hoisting a prodigious six off Bicknell which whistled past the scoreboard and into a
garden. Soon a box of balls was being brought out from the pavilion from which Surrey
and the umpires were able to select one of similar age and wear.

The *cognoscenti* on the county circuit assert that playing Surrey is as near as one gets
to Test cricket without actually taking part. While the England side were performing
appallingly at Lord's, the tough and competitive Sussex side were playing highly skilful
cricket and, in the course of the afternoon, they reduced the County Champions to 126
for six. James Kirtley soon trapped Ian Ward on the back foot and Batty went to a head-
high catch by Tim Ambrose behind the stumps. Graham Thorpe looked a different class
from anyone else, but a brilliant catch at square leg by Davis sent him packing. Mushtaq
and Martin-Jenkins then did some serious damage to the Surrey middle order, and it was
left to Mark Ramprakash, who started slowly but again revealed a fine technique, to join

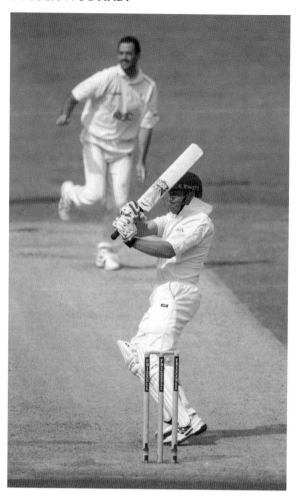

Left Chris Adams powerfully hooks Martin Bicknell of Surrey, later to be recalled to England colours for the Fourth Test against South Africa.

Opposite James Kirtley, shortly to make his Test debut for England against South Africa, bowls against Surrey at Hove.

with Bicknell and add an unbroken 86 by the close. They would still need another 68 to avoid the follow-on on the Friday morning.

Mushtaq struck early on the next morning and, in the course of three balls, sent back Bicknell and Salisbury, but then the wheels came off the Sussex attack. Ramprakash went on steadily to a five-hour hundred before falling to Kirtley's first delivery with the second new ball, while Saqlain lashed at everything as he struck eight fours and three sixes, adding 84 in 20 overs with the patient Ramprakash and then, annoyingly for Sussex, a further 54 for the last wicket with the ebullient Ormond. Surrey, who might well have followed-on at one stage, scrambled their way to only 74 runs behind Sussex. Losing Montgomerie early on, Sussex appeared unwilling to take the initiative, although Tony Cottey made a brisk 41. Adams and Goodwin, however, seemed to be in defensive mode and, when they were offered the light, which was murky but by no means unplayable, they accepted it readily. They were then 143 in front with eight wickets left and 37 overs in the day to go. Murmurs, possibly uninformed ones, in the pavilion such as 'Do they really want to win the Championship?' seemed to abound.

The murky light of the previous day had not improved on the Saturday morning. Goodwin – with a dislocated finger caused during fielding practice – and Adams carried on where they had left off, but when both were back in the smart new players' area attached to the new indoor school and the score was only 108 for four, Sussex were just 182 runs on with 80 overs still to go. As it happened they need not have worried. Ambrose took root and moved to his eighth half-century of the season, adding 120 with Martin-Jenkins for the 5th wicket before Matt Prior bludgeoned a 49-ball 50. Ten minutes before tea Adams declared on 302 for five, leaving Surrey a notional 377 in 36 overs. Hardly bright cricket, of course, but the matter was diplomatically glossed over by the award of county caps to Ambrose and Prior during the tea interval. Long before this, however, Surrey had lost interest as Saqlain and Salisbury essayed some odd medium-pace and Hollioake tried to remember whether he could bowl leg-spin. In their second innings Surrey pottered on to 114 for the loss of Ian Ward's wicket before the match closed with nobody feeling satisfied.

Post-match headlines, such as 'Strutting Surrey scare off Sussex' and 'Edgy Sussex let Surrey off the hook', were everywhere and may just have had a tiny grain of truth. Yet it was not perhaps quite fair on Chris Adams. While the decision to take the light with 37 overs remaining on the Friday afternoon might have been seen as questionable, few people had considered that Surrey have some of the best bowlers in county cricket and a side that can bat in depth. On the murky Saturday morning the situation had not fundamentally altered. Peter Moores was adamant that Adams had made some good decisions: 'The light was bad,' he said. 'It was the captain's decision. He did not wish to expose the middle order, especially when Murray Goodwin was already struggling with a dislocated finger.' Adams himself also had something to say to *The Argus:* 'Surrey would have expected to come here and dominate us, even though we are second, but we have gone at them and dominated them for four days. On Saturday morning there were a lot of verbals flying around, but I take that as a good sign!'

Sussex, trailing Surrey by five points at the start, ended up one fewer behind. Had they won, they would have opened up a ten-point lead. Had they lost, however, Surrey would have increased their lead to 18 points. In any case, who *did* win the Championship?

Sussex (12 points) drew with Surrey (11 points).

SUSSEX v SURREY

at Hove on 30th July - 2nd August - Frizzell County Championship Division 1

* Captain, + Wicket-Keeper

Sussex won the toss and elected to bat

MATCH BALL SPONSORS
Roger & Annie Hancock

SUSSEX

#	Batsman	1st Innings			2nd Innings	
1	R.R. Montgomerie [7]	b: Salisbury	90		Lbw b: Bicknell	2
2	M.W. Goodwin [3]	b: Ormond	75		c: Ward b: Saqlain	29
3	P.A. Cottey [2]	Lbw b: Saqlain	1		c: Ramprakash b: Mahmood	41
4	C.J. Adams * [1]	c: Batty b: Ormond	107		Lbw b: Saqlain	23
5	T.R. Ambrose + [11]	c: Mahmood b: Salisbury	43		not out	76
6	R.S.C. Martin-Jenkins [12]	b: Bicknell	40		b: Salisbury	45
7	M.J. Prior [13]	c: Thorpe b: Ormond	0		not out	50
8	M.J.G. Davis [8]	c: Clarke b: Ormond	0			
9	Mushtaq Ahmed [9]	c: Batty b: Mahmood	26			
10	R.J. Kirtley [6]	(11) not out	1			
11	P.M. Hutchison [23]	(10) c: Ward b: Bicknell	5			
12	B.V. Taylor [22]					

					Extras									Extras	
b 6	lb 13	wd 0	nb 22	Extras	41			b 9	lb 8	wd 0	nb 14	Extras	36		
Overs	126	Provisional Total	429					Overs	87.5	Provisional Total	302				
Pens	0	Wkts	10	Total	429			Pens	5	Wkts	5 dec	Total	302		

Fall of wickets:
1st Inns: 1-149 2-150 3-232 4-330 5-363 6-363 7-367 8-415 9-423 10-429
2nd Inns: 1-7 2-67 3-89 4-108 5-228

Bonus Points - Sussex 5, Surrey 3

Bowling	Ovs	Md	R	Wk	wd	nb	Ovs	Md	R	Wk	wd	nb
Bicknell	26	5	94	2	0	3	16	5	54	1	0	2
Ormond	25	6	106	4	0	0	10	3	17	0	0	0
Hollioake	7	3	23	0	0	0	0.5	0	11	0	0	1
Mahmood	18	5	61	1	0	3	4	1	3	1	0	0
Saqlain	36	5	84	1	0	5	35	7	97	2	0	4
Salisbury	14	0	42	2	0	0	22	0	98	1	0	0

SURREY — 1st Innings / 2nd Innings — Target 377

#	Batsman	1st Innings			2nd Innings	
1	I.J. Ward	Lbw b: Kirtley	20		Lbw b: Davis	33
2	J.N. Batty +	c: Ambrose b: Hutchison	12		not out	65
3	M.R. Ramprakash	c: Ambrose b: Kirtley	104		not out	14
4	G.P. Thorpe	c: Davis b: Martin-Jenkins	23			
5	J. Ormond	(11) not out	42			
6	R. Clarke	(5) c: Mushtaq b: Martin-Jenkins	12			
7	A.J. Hollioake *	(6) Lbw b: Mushtaq	13			
8	Azhar Mahmood	(7) Lbw b: Mushtaq	9			
9	M.P. Bicknell	(8) Lbw b: Mushtaq	42			
10	I.D.K. Salisbury	(9) st: Ambrose b: Mushtaq	1			
11	Saqlain Mushtaq	(10) b: Martin-Jenkins	68			
12	A.D. Brown					

					Extras									Extras	
b 1	lb 6	wd 0	nb 2	Extras	9			b 0	lb 2	wd 0	nb 0	Extras	2		
Overs	102.3	Provisional Total	355					Overs	26	Provisional Total	114				
Pens	0	Wkts	10	Total	355			Pens	0	Wkts	1	Total	114		

Fall of wickets:
1st Inns: 1-32 2-32 3-75 4-89 5-116 6-126 7-215 8-215 9-301 10-355
2nd Inns: 1-82

Bonus Points - Surrey 4, Sussex 3

Bowling	Ovs	Md	R	Wk	wd	nb	Ovs	Md	R	Wk	wd	nb
Kirtley	28	4	90	2	0	0	6	1	23	0	0	0
Hutchison	16	2	58	1	0	1	7	1	30	0	0	0
Mushtaq	38	7	123	4	0	0	6	1	26	0	0	0
Martin-Jenkins	17.3	3	67	3	0	0	3	0	17	0	0	0
Davis	3	0	10	0	0	0	4	1	16	1	0	0

MATCH DRAWN

CLUB SPONSORS 2003
OFFICIAL CLUB SPONSOR:
P@v - i.t. services
SPONSORS:
ACCELERATED MAILING
ALLFIELD FINANCIAL GROUP
BAKER TILLY
CHARCOL
ERADICATION & CLEANING
FAMILY ASSURANCE
FINN CRISP
GILES CONTRACTS MGMT LTD
GRAND CRU GROUP
MISHON MACKAY
PSE ASSOCIATES
RENDEZVOUS CASINO
RIVERVALE
SETYRES
SHEPHERD NEAME
SOLV IT
TATES
THE SUPPORTERS CLUB
VOKINS @ HOME
WYNDEHAM PRESS GRP
WYNNE BAXTER

UMPIRES :
M.R. Benson
M.J. Harris

SCORERS :
J.F. Hartridge
C.J. Hamm

HOURS OF PLAY
Days 1 - 3: 11am - 6.30pm
Day 4: 11am - 6pm
Lunch
Days 1 - 3: 1.15pm - 1.55pm
Day 4: 1pm - 1.40pm
Tea
Days 1 - 3: 4.10pm - 4.30pm
or when 32 overs remain to be bowled, whichever is later
Day 4: 3.40pm - 4pm

1st Inns Bonus Pts
(Only in the first 130 Overs)
Batting (Max 5pts)
1pt at achieving 200, 250, 300, 350 and 400 runs.
Bowling (Max 3pts)
1 pt for taking 3, 6 & 9 wkts

SUSSEX v. LANCASHIRE AT HOVE
Thursday to Sunday, 14 to 17 August 2003

When Sussex decided to play cannily for a draw against Surrey in the previous Championship match they must have known that they twice had to face Lancashire, one of the three top sides, in the final run-in, whereas Surrey had a rather easier path. On balance, however, they probably had made the right decision. In the 2002 season Chris Adams had taken a double-hundred off the Lancashire bowlers at Old Trafford and, on winning the toss for the third time running, he must have known that his own form would be a principal ingredient of any success.

The start of the Sussex innings was anything but propitious, as Murray Goodwin and Tony Cottey both succumbed early. John Wood found the edge of Goodwin's bat, while Cottey cut to point off Kyle Hogg, the player nominated to stand down if Glen Chapple returned from the Trent Bridge Test. This brought in Adams to join Richard Montgomerie who, after a 3rd-wicket stand of 72 with his skipper, edged Peter Martin to first slip. He had made 72, only his fourth half-century in 20 innings. Adams, however, fresh from his first hundred of the season against Surrey and relishing the short boundary on the pavilion side and the speed of the brown outfield, was in dominant form. In Gary Keedy's first over of left-arm spin he struck him straight for six and then hit fours through extra cover and fine on the leg side. He was given adequate support by Tim Ambrose and Robin Martin-Jenkins, but the rest of the middle order which had been serving Sussex so well throughout much of the season failed to ignite and, when Matt Prior was out, seven wickets were down for 257. Adams, who can seldom be accused of failing to make runs on important occasions, regained the initiative in the company of Mushtaq, reaching his century off 150 balls in the over before tea.

Glen Chapple, unlike James Kirtley on this occasion at least, was found surplus to England's requirements and arrived from Nottingham in the course of the afternoon. His long journey had obviously done him no good, because he went for 27 runs from his first three overs and for 48 from seven, while failing to catch Mushtaq at mid-off. Runs were now coming thick and fast, but when Warren Hegg brought on Chris Schofield, the leg-spinner who once had an England contract but who nowadays does not always find a place in the Lancashire side, he immediately took two wickets in one over. Adams, after a 191-ball stay for 140 with five sixes and 16 fours, was pinned lbw on the back foot by a googly and Hutchison went the same way. Mushtaq, however, was enjoying himself and he and Billy Taylor added 53 for the last wicket before the Pakistani wizard perished for 60, his highest score for Sussex.

Lancashire, who had survived four overs on the previous evening, batted soundly on the Friday morning without ever showing the belligerence that Adams and Mushtaq had produced the previous day. Mark Chilton and Iain Sutcliffe missed a century opening stand by one run and, when they and Mal Loye were out for 150, the Lancashire innings was held together by Stuart Law. He eventually found a reliable partner in Chapple who, it must be said, batted very much better than he had bowled on the Thursday. Mushtaq, however, was possibly overbowled by Adams, but such was the Pakistani's effect that this was understandable. He started at the Sea End on account of the short boundary on the pavilion side, but during the afternoon he was switched to the Cromwell Road End

Richard Montgomerie, the scorer of two 70s in the match with Lancashire at Hove in mid-August, bats thoughtfully on the first day.

where there was apparently more turn but a greater chance of being swept to the boundary. Throughout the day, however, he bamboozled all the Lancashire batsmen, including Law and Carl Hooper, probably the best combination at numbers 4 and 5 on the county circuit. Hooper, in attempting to pull Mushtaq to the short leg-side boundary skied a catch to the bowler, while Law was taken in the leg trap just four short of his hundred. When the close came Lancashire, who at one stage might have faced a follow-on, had moved to 351 for eight and Mushtaq had completed 43 overs with an economy rate of 2.58 and taken four good wickets as well. On an intrinsically sound batting pitch against an excellent batting side this was no mean achievement for a wrist-spinner.

A stoutly struck 30 from John Wood brought his side to within eight runs of the Sussex total, so after two innings there was really everything to play for. Sussex's second knock began disastrously with Goodwin and Cottey out with only two on the board, but Montgomerie made a second 70 in a 153-run stand with Adams, whose return to form had coincided with the end of Cottey's purple patch. Strangely perhaps, Adams batted quietly and reached his 50 in 137 balls whereas Montgomerie, not noted for any attacking propensities, had achieved his half-century in 20 balls fewer. With the demise

Chris Adams acknowledges his hundred on the way to 140 in his first innings against Lancashire at Hove.

of Montgomerie, Adams settled down with Ambrose to add a further 110, leaving Sussex 273 ahead with seven wickets remaining at the close.

The final day belonged to Adams, Taylor and Mushtaq. The Sussex captain knew that he needed to make a canny declaration if he was to build on the advantage that his own second innings had achieved. He must have been mindful that he had been criticised – largely unfairly – for being over-cautious in the Surrey match, but an over-generous declaration against Law and Hooper with a short boundary would give any captain pause for thought. Adams went on from 147 overnight to 190 before he returned a catch to Chapple, while Prior hit out fiercely so that Lancashire were set 392 to win off a minimum of 75 overs. On this occasion Mushtaq was not really the match winner, although he did take five wickets. Rather it was Taylor who bowled as well as he could ever have done. He removed both openers and then, extracting extra bounce from the Cromwell Road End, he caused both Law and Hooper into misjudgements so that both were caught by Adams at slip. Mushtaq, by dint of vociferous appealing as only he knows how, won three lbws in the final stages and with only 12 minutes of the final hour left – possibly time for four more overs – Sussex won the day. Mushtaq, who had confided to Peter Moores over Saturday lunch that he felt he was on for 100 wickets in

Opposite Chris Adams cuts to the boundary on the way to 190 (and 330 runs in the match) against Lancashire.

the season, for the 8th time took five or more wickets in an innings and brought his tally to 82 – with four matches to go a century of wickets looked like no idle threat, while Taylor's four wickets for 42 runs off 26 overs was a highly significant contribution. In many ways, however, in the course of this important and exciting win by Sussex it was the captain who enjoyed the greatest personal triumph. His 190 with 21 fours in the second innings meant that he had a match total of 330 runs, made in the course of ten hours and 16 minutes of controlled batting power.

After the match Peter Moores, director of Sussex cricket, spoke about his side's achievement and, in particular about Adams and Mushtaq. 'Good players have three assets – great will, persistence and huge belief,' he said. 'Chris until recently had lost a bit of belief. He played two great innings and the second was the best I have ever seen him bat.' In the same vein he noted about Mushtaq: 'He is hungry to prove that he is still one of the world's best even though Pakistan aren't picking him. He gives us belief. Our game is institutionalised; he's a reminder you need not be that way.'

Sussex (21 points) beat Lancashire (7 points) by 252 runs.

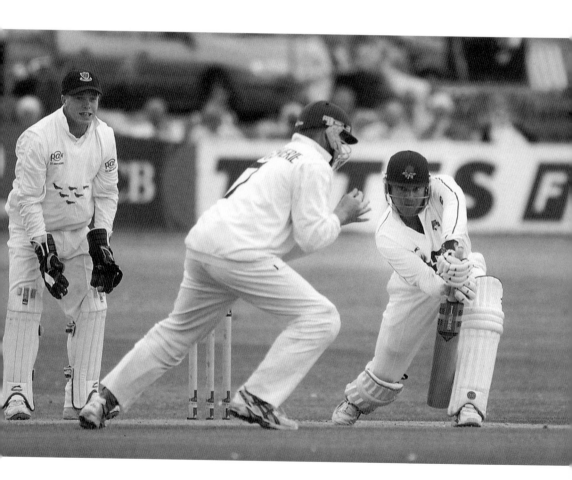

SUSSEX v LANCASHIRE

at Hove on 14th - 17th August - Frizzell County Championship Division 1

Sussex won the toss and elected to bat

* Captain, + Wicket-Keeper

SUSSEX

#	Batsman	1st innings		2nd innings	
1	R.R. Montgomerie [7]	c: Law b: Martin	72	c: Sutcliffe b: Martin	70
2	M.W. Goodwin [3]	c: Hegg b: Wood	9	c: Sutcliffe b: Martin	1
3	P.A. Cottey [2]	c: Schofield b: Hogg	18	c: Hegg b: Martin	0
4	C.J. Adams * [1]	lbw b: Schofield	140	ct & b: Chapple	190
5	T.R. Ambrose + [11]	c: Sutcliffe b: Wood	18	ct & b: Chapple	44
6	R.S.C. Martin-Jenkins [12]	c: Law b: Wood	18	Lbw b: Chapple	13
7	M.J. Prior [13]	c: Hegg b: Keedy	9	not out	35
8	M.J.G. Davis [8]	Lbw b: Hooper	3	not out	16
9	Mushtaq Ahmed [9]	Lbw b: Schofield	60		
10	P.M. Hutchison [23]	Lbw b: Schofield	0		
11	B.V. Taylor [22]	not out	13		
12					

b 8	lb 6	wd 1	nb 10	Extras	25	b 2	lb 8	wd 0	nb 4	Extras	14
Overs			100.3	Provisional Total	385	Overs			104.4	Provisional Total	383
Pens		0	Wkts	Total	385	Pens		0	Wkts	Total	383
			10						7		

Fall of wickets
1st Inns: 1 - 12 2 - 60 3 - 132 4 -156 5 -190 6 -252 7 -257 8 -332 9 -332 10-385
2nd Inns: 1 - 2 2 - 2 3 -155 4 -268 5 -313 6 -348 7 -383

Bonus Points - Sussex 4, Lancs 3

Bowling

Bowling	Ovs	Md	R	Wk	wd	nb	Ovs	Md	R	Wk	wd	nb
Martin	15	2	64	1	0	1	21	5	61	3	0	0
Wood	17	2	64	3	0	3	17.4	2	72	1	0	1
Chilton	12	2	33	0	1	0	-	-	-	-	-	-
Hogg	8	2	24	1	0	1						
Keedy	24	6	76	1	0	0	19	3	61	0	0	0
Hooper	12	2	48	1	0	0	22	4	65	0	0	0
Chapple	7	0	48	0	0	0	21	3	89	3	0	1
Schofield	5.3	2	14	3	0	0	4	0	25	0	0	0

LANCASHIRE

#	Batsman	1st innings			2nd innings		
1	M.J. Chilton [21]		c: Montgomerie b: Davis	65		b: Taylor	9
2	I.J. Sutcliffe [5]		c: Prior b: Mushtaq	43		c: Montgomerie b: Taylor	12
3	M.B. Loye [1]		c: Goodwin b: Taylor	2		Lbw b: Mushtaq	33
4	S.G. Law [2]		c: Montgomerie b: Mushtaq	96		c: Adams b: Taylor	7
5	C.L. Hooper [17]		ct & b: Mushtaq	23		c: Adams b: Taylor	1
6	C.P. Schofield [15]		b: Mushtaq	3		b: Davis	18
7	W.K. Hegg [10] * +	(8)	c: Montgomerie b: Mushtaq	31	(8)	c: Montgomerie b: Mushtaq	25
8	P.J. Martin [24]	(9)	b: Taylor	9	(9)	c: Prior b: Mushtaq	0
9	G. Chapple [3]	(7)	c: Goodwin b: Taylor	54	(7)	Lbw b: Mushtaq	7
10	J. Wood [7]		Lbw b: Mushtaq	30		Lbw b: Mushtaq	0
11	G. Keedy [23]		not out	0		not out	2
12	K.W. Hogg [22]						

b 10	lb 3	wd 0	nb 8	Extras	21	b 6	lb 7	wd 0	nb 12	Extras	25
Overs			121	Provisional Total	377	Overs			73.2	Provisional Total	139
Pens		0	Wkts	Total	377	Pens		0	Wkts	Total	139
			10						10		

Fall of wickets
1st Inns: 1 - 99 2 -102 3 -150 4 -189 5 -192 6 -289 7 -307 8 -321 9 -358 10-377
2nd Inns: 1 - 27 2 - 28 3 - 56 4 - 64 5 - 97 6 -109 7 -128 8 -132 9 -132 10-139

Bonus Points - Lancs 4, Sussex 3

Bowling

Bowling	Ovs	Md	R	Wk	wd	nb	Ovs	Md	R	Wk	wd	nb
Hutchison	14	2	50	0	0	0	2	0	20	0	0	3
Taylor	24	8	56	3	0	4	26	12	42	4	0	3
Mushtaq Ahmed	48	10	124	6	0	0	33.2	14	49	5	0	0
Martin-Jenkins	9	1	48	0	0	0	-	-	-	-	-	-
Davis	26	2	86	1	0	0	12	6	15	1	0	0

SUSSEX WON BY 252 RUNS

Opposite Richard Montgomerie catches Lancashire captain Warren Hegg off Mushtaq as Sussex move in for the kill at Hove.

SUSSEX v. ESSEX AT COLCHESTER

Wednesday to Friday, 20 to 22 August, 2003

Castle Park, the beautiful tree-ringed ground in Colchester, is apparently under threat. Essex are not sure whether they are able to sustain what is, in effect, a Colchester Festival unless they receive support from the local council, who seem reluctant to be forthcoming. Gold may not be running into the Essex coffers, but for Sussex and, more especially for Murray Goodwin, the opening day was one of golden cricket.

The experts noted that the pitch had been left well-grassed, presumably to counter the effects of Mushtaq, whose wizardry was now striking fear into the hearts of counties the length and breadth of England. Fortunately for Sussex, the Essex attack had no idea how to use such a pitch, and Goodwin and Richard Montgomerie put on 161 before lunch. After the interval Tony Palladino caused Montgomerie, who had been the main aggressor and had reached 83 in the morning session, to drag a ball on to his leg stump when he had made 97 off 133 balls and the Sussex total had risen to 202 in a mere 45 overs. In the afternoon it was all Goodwin, who made 101 in the session, although many Sussex batsmen missed out. Tony Cottey was sent back by Goodwin and run out, Chris Adams yorked first ball and Tim Ambrose and Robin Martin-Jenkins did not stay long. Goodwin reached his second hundred of the season off 151 balls and needed a mere 34 more to complete 150 as he returned to his very best form. Matt Prior complemented Goodwin and, by driving Graham Napier for successive sixes, he moved effortlessly from 89 to his hundred. In the meantime, after nearly six hours' batting, Goodwin succumbed for 210, his highest first-class score, made from 270 balls with 30 fours and two sixes. Sussex's score of 521 for eight at the close off 104 overs – a rate of fractionally more than five runs per over – was the result of good cricket, although it must be said, in truth, that Essex, staring down the barrel at relegation, had bowled poorly. One front-line bowler went for over six an over, two other regulars well in excess of five – only Palladino, who kept it reasonably tight, and Mohammad Akram, who turned no wicket for 70 into five for 98 at the close, were possible exceptions.

If Essex thought that their torture was close to its end on the second morning they were wholly in error. Prior, moving down the wicket to meet the bowling and hitting straight down the ground, reached the first 150 of his career, which included 19 fours and three sixes off only 134 balls. The 9th-wicket pair of Prior and Jason Lewry, who made the first fifty of his long career, added 141 in only 19 overs.

It is a good side that takes the sort of battering that Essex had received and responds in kind when their turn to bat comes. The openers, Will Jefferson and Darren Robinson, both deceived by Mushtaq after they had each passed 50, made 101 together, but only Zimbabwean Andy Flower, who three times reverse-swept Mushtaq for four, looked really solid. When he was dismissed there was some desultory resistance from James Foster, James Middlebrook and Graham Napier, but Mushtaq added four scalps to his ever increasing total and Mark Davis chipped in with his off-spin to take two good

Opposite Murray Goodwin completed the second double-hundred of his career at the Castle ground in Colchester during the match with Essex in late August.

wickets when the maestro grew tired. Since Palladino was unable to bat and the fall of the 9th wicket saw the end of the Essex innings, Chris Adams had no hesitation in enforcing the follow-on.

The prospect of a Saturday crowd swelling the Essex coffers came to nought as the Sussex juggernaut moved on during the Friday. Off the fourth ball of the morning an athletic Chris Adams ran out the over-enthusiastic Robinson and although Jefferson, who had batted well in the first innings, again passed 50 and looked good, engaging in a 2nd-wicket stand of 85 with Flower, there was little else to commend in the Essex innings apart from a dogged 38 from skipper Ronnie Irani. Mushtaq had bowled 53 overs for his seven wickets in the match and was understandably tired, so it was left to Billy Taylor, who often went through the top of the less than perfect pitch and made some balls rear awkwardly, to tidy up the Essex innings at 3.50 p.m.

Peter Moores, director of cricket, was understandably pleased with the result when he spoke after the match to *The Kent and Sussex Courier*: 'We are playing some very good cricket at the moment. We have scored our runs pretty quickly all year and, first up in a match, you want to score or take wickets quickly to give yourselves a platform for a win. Murray, Monty and Matt all did very well for us in the way they scored their runs.'

Sussex (22 points) beat Essex (5 points) by an innings and 120 runs.

Essex CCC v Sussex CCC at Castle Park, Colchester on 20, 21, 22 & 23 August 2003 DAY 4

Result: Sussex (22pts) beat Essex (5pts) by an innings and 120 runs

Essex — 1st Innings

Essex	How Out	Bowler	Total
1 D D J Robinson	c Cottey	Mushtaq Ahmed	64
2 W I Jefferson	c Goodwin	Mushtaq Ahmed	55
3 A Flower	c Ambrose	Lewry	50
4 A Habib	lbw	Mushtaq Ahmed	0
5 R C Irani *	c Adams	Taylor	3
6 J S Foster +	c Montgomerie	Davis	31
7 J M Dakin	lbw	Davis	6
8 J D Middlebrook	c Lewry	Martin-Jenkins	33
9 G R Napier	c Prior	Mushtaq Ahmed	34
10 M Akram	not out		0
11 A P Palladino	injured		

Bonus Pts	b	lb	w	nb	p		Extras	Total
	0	5	0	2	0		7	283

Fall of Wicket	1	2	3	4	5	6	7	8	9	10
Score at Fall	101	144	144	163	208	219	281	283		

Bowling	O	M	R	W	wd	nb
LEWRY	12.0	4	46	1	0	0
TAYLOR	17.0	3	52	2	0	0
MUSHTAQ AHMED	25.0	2	87	4	0	0
MARTIN-JENKINS	11.5	2	32	1	0	0
DAVIS	12.0	0	61	2	0	1

Essex — 2nd Innings

Essex	How Out	Bowler	Total
1 D D J Robinson	run out		12
2 W I Jefferson	c & b	Martin-Jenkins	59
3 A Flower	c Prior	Mushtaq Ahmed	32
4 A Habib	bowled	Mushtaq Ahmed	11
5 R C Irani	c Ambrose	Taylor	38
6 J S Foster	lbw	Mushtaq Ahmed	3
7 J M Dakin	c Goodwin	Taylor	7
8 J D Middlebrook	c Davis	Taylor	5
9 G R Napier	not out		21
10 M Akram	lbw	Taylor	10

Bonus Pts	b	lb	w	nb		Extras	Total
	2	3	0	6		11	209

Fall of Wicket	1	2	3	4	5	6	7	8	9	10
Score at Fall	24	109	123	130	164	154	172	185	209	

Sussex — 1st Innings

Sussex	How Out	Bowler	Total
1 R R Montgomerie	bowled	Palladino	97
2 M W Goodwin	bowled	Akram	210
3 P A Cottey	run out		23
4 C J Adams *	bowled	Akram	0
5 T R Ambrose +	bowled	Akram	4
6 R S C Martin-Jenkins	c Flower	Middlebrook	10
7 M J Prior	not out		153
8 M J G Davis	bowled	Akram	8
9 Mushtaq Ahmed	bowled	Akram	0
10 J D Lewry	c Sub	Middlebrook	70
11 B V Taylor	bowled	Dakin	3

Bonus Pts	b	lb	w	nb	p		Extras	Total
	0	9	0	20	5		34	612

Fall of Wicket	1	2	3	4	5	6	7	8	9	10
Score at Fall	202	270	270	303	325	430	452	454	595	612

Bowling	O	M	R	W	wd	nb
AKRAM	29.0	2	130	5	0	5
DAKIN	20.0	1	120	1	0	2
NAPIER	24.0	5	149	5	0	2
PALLADINO	16.0	6	40	1	0	0
MIDDLEBROOK	26.0	1	126	2	0	0
ROBINSON	4.0	0	33	0	0	1

Sussex — 2nd Innings

(not required)

Scorers: A E Choat & J F Hartridge

Umpires: N J Llong and A Clarkson

Toss: Sussex won the toss and chose to bat

* Captain   + Wicketkeeper

INTERVAL TIMES

Lunch Time: 1.15 - 1.35pm   Tea Time: 4.10pm - 4.30pm
(4th day) 1.10 - 1.40pm   (4th day) 3.40pm - 4.00pm

Provided that at tea interval 20 overs or less remains to be bowled (not 4th day). Tea interval changes of 9 wickets down, play will continue for 8 overs or 30 runs, whichever is the later or after the conclusion of the current innings.

All interval times in September scheduled for 30 minutes earlier.

BONUS POINTS

Awarded in the first 130 overs of each first innings.

Batting: 200-249 runs 1pt   Bowling: 3-5 wickets 1pt
250-299 runs 2pts   6-8 wickets 2pts
300-349 runs 3pts   9-10 wickets 3pts
350-399 runs 4pts
400 runs plus 5pts

14 Points for a win, 6 points for a tie, 4 points for a draw

HOURS OF PLAY

1st, 2nd & 3rd Days: 11am - 6.30pm (10.30am-6pm in September) or after 104 overs have been bowled, whichever is the later.

4th Day: 11am-6pm (10.30am - 5.30pm in September) or after 96 overs have been bowled, whichever is the later.

In a change of innings, 2 overs will be deducted from the minimum number of overs to be bowled plus any over in progress at the end of the completed innings.

If play is suspended (including interval) between innings) the minimum overs to be bowled in the day shall be reduced by one over for each full 3 minutes 45 secs of the aggregate playing time lost. If, at 5pm on the 4th day (4.30pm in September) 16 overs or less remain to be bowled, the Umpires shall indicate that play shall continue until a minimum of a further 16 overs have been bowled or 6pm (5.30pm) whichever is later, provided a result is not reached earlier. If, however, at 5.30pm (5pm) both Captains (the batsmen at the wicket may act for their Captain) accept that there is no prospect of a result to the match to any further first innings bonus points, they may agree to cease play at that time. Such agreement may be reached at anytime after 5.30pm (5pm in September).

LEAGUE TABLES 2003

Sussex must have been mindful of the disaster that struck them when they played Middlesex in the first match of the season at Lord's. Setting their opponents the highest total of the match to win, they had allowed Middlesex to reach 328 and snatch victory in a match that Sussex should never have lost, even though the Lord's pitch apparently flattened out in the later stages of the game.

Middlesex's winning of the toss on a perfect morning for cricket was certainly tempered by Jason Lewry, who removed Sven Koenig and Ben Hutton for ten runs in the course of nine hostile overs, but after that – at least for most of the day – it was all Middlesex. Andrew Strauss, the visitors' captain and a batsman tipped for England's winter tours, together with Owais Shah, now apparently discarded by the England hierarchy, settled into a productive partnership for the 3rd wicket of 219 in 46 overs. Once the new ball had lost its hardness the Sussex seam trio of Lewry, Billy Taylor and Robin Martin-Jenkins found it difficult work, and it was left to Mushtaq, brought on as early as the 18th over, to make the batsmen think. For all his wizardry, however, and despite the fact that a perfectly pitched leg-break missed Shah's outside edge and his off stump by the traditional fag paper when he was on 22, Mushtaq was unable to break through. Strauss appeared able to read him out of the hand and swept and pulled him forcefully, while Shah, quick on his feet, played him elegantly off the pitch. The exit of Strauss, caught by Prior off a leading edge for a well-made hundred, started the unravelling of the Middlesex innings. Mushtaq, after his morning spell, had been brought on immediately after lunch and continued through until the close. He did not take a wicket until the 74th over, during which time he had bowled 26 overs and conceded 113 runs. He then proceeded to have Shah and Ed Joyce lbw and to dismantle the rest of the Middlesex innings so that the last five wickets went down for 18 runs in 27 balls, while his six wickets brought him to 95 for the season. On a good wicket Sussex had claimed the three bowling points which were likely to be crucial in the final run-in.

Middlesex have not won at Hove since 1990 and Sussex's record at home in the current season was intact, but when the home side were 87 for five at lunch the pavilion talk was all of Sussex fluffing their lines at the vital moment. The morning had begun sultry and dull and the Sussex top order seemed all awry in the face of some good seam bowling by Chad Keegan and Joe Dawes. Murray Goodwin was lbw offering no shot, Richard Montgomerie, having been missed two balls previously, guided one to the 'keeper and Chris Adams, perhaps not for the first time, was caught behind off an ill-judged drive. Tony Cottey had come to the wicket requiring one Championship run for his 1,000 and, although he achieved this, he perished soon afterwards.

Not long after lunch Sussex had lost six wickets for 107 and the prospect of being made to follow-on was a real possibility, but Matt Prior and Mark Davis (is there a better number 8 on the county circuit?) were made of sterner stuff. While Prior made an array of attacking shots as the sun emerged from the clouds and lightened the field, Davis hung in gamely and occasionally lashed a ball to the boundary. At tea they were still together and all thoughts of a follow-on had been dispelled. When the partnership had added 195 priceless runs Prior top-edged a sweep and departed for 148 made off just

Above Sussex players congratulate Jason Lewry after he has bowled Middlesex opener Sven Koenig on the first day of Sussex's match with Middlesex at Hove in early September. *Below* Mushtaq appeals vociferously, but unsuccessfully, against Middlesex captain Andrew Strauss at Hove.

153 balls with 25 boundaries to his credit. It was now left to Davis, who had now started to blossom and was three short of his own ton at the close, and the mischievous Mushtaq, who clattered a 53-ball half-century, to guide the County to 401 for eight and the full five batting points. This great recovery was enhanced by the news that Surrey had crashed to Kent at Canterbury and had scored a paltry three points.

On the Sunday morning 401 for eight playing 392 all out looked a little like even-steven, but that was not the scenario envisaged by Davis. Batting altogether for a total of seven-and-a-half hours, he added 32 with Lewry and then partnered Taylor in a last-wicket stand of 106 in 40 overs. Strangely, number 11 Taylor, whose 35 was his highest first-class score, faced 146 balls, that is to say, 60% of the strike while he and Davis were together. When Davis, generally regarded as a bowling all-rounder, was eventually out for an splendid 168, the last four Sussex wickets had added 430 runs and Sussex's 537 looked impressive. Many correspondents recognised this as evidence of huge self-belief in a well-moulded and committed team who were intent on winning the Championship.

Facing a deficit of 145, Middlesex lost their skipper when Strauss nicked the sixth ball of the innings to Ambrose. Worse was to follow: Koenig was undone by a yorker from Martin-Jenkins and Hutton caught at long leg. When Mushtaq was brought on he probed the batsmen's weaknesses and bowled Joyce with a flipper, while Shah, not mindful of the approaching close of play, tried the charge at Davis and was left stranded. With a mere 12-run lead and five wickets lost, Middlesex looked in real danger.

The cards were stacked against the visitors, but Middlesex managed to lose only two wickets in the morning session, both to Lewry who trapped Peploe lbw and caused Nash to play on. Things moved on rapidly after lunch as Mushtaq took three wickets in successive overs, including that of the dogged Paul Weekes who had batted tenaciously for three hours before Prior snapped him at silly point. This was Mushtaq's fifth ten-wicket match haul of the season and left him, tantalisingly, on 99 for the season.

Sussex, needing 106 to take the match, lost Goodwin and Cottey, both lbw to Dawes, before a 70-run partnership between Adams and Montgomerie either side of the tea interval virtually sealed the match. Adams was dismissed off bat and pad in the first over after tea, but Montgomerie and Ambrose saw the County home with 22 overs still in hand. As the pair walked off there were strains of 'Sussex by the Sea' from many parts of the ground. It seemed that Sussex, needing a mere ten points from two matches, were about to clinch the title.

Chris Adams, who with Peter Moores had nurtured a marvellous dressing-room spirit, was full of praise for his side. 'Mushtaq has been brilliant,' he told *The Times,* 'but it has really been a massive team effort.'

Sussex (22 points) beat Middlesex (7 points) by seven wickets.

Opposite Matt Prior's 148 averted a first-innings collapse against Middlesex and led finally to a convincing victory.

SUSSEX v MIDDLESEX

at Hove on 5th - 8th September - Frizzell County Championship Division 1

Middlesex won the toss and elected to bat

*Captain, + Wicket-Keeper

SUSSEX

#	Batsman	1st Innings		2nd Innings (Target 106)	
1	M.W. Goodwin [3]	Lbw b: Dawes	14	Lbw b: Dawes	4
2	R.R. Montgomerie [7]	c: Nash b: Dawes	21	not out	54
3	P.A. Cottey [2]	c: Hutton b: Keegan	15	Lbw b: Dawes	7
4	C.J. Adams * [1]	c: Nash b: Cook	20	c: Hutton b: Weekes	30
5	T.R. Ambrose + [11]	c: Hutton b: Keegan	12	not out	11
6	R.S.C. Martin-Jenkins [12]	c: Hutton b: Dawes	8		
7	M.J. Prior [13]	c: Shah b: Weekes	148		
8	M.J.G. Davis [8]	c: Dawes B: Keegan	168		
9	Mushtaq Ahmed [9]	c: Shah b: Weekes	57		
10	J.D. Lewry [5]	c: Peploe b: Keegan	21		
11	B.V. Taylor [22]	not out	35		
12	C.D. Hopkinson [21]				

	1st Innings			2nd Innings		
Extras	b 5	lb 2	wd 7	nb 4	Extras	18
Extras	b 1	lb 1	wd 0	nb 0	Extras	2
Overs	152.2		Provisional Total	537		
Overs	27.5		Provisional Total	108		
Pens	0	Wkts	10	Total	537	
Pens	0	Wkts	3	Total	108	

Fall of wickets 1st Inns: 1-26 2-37 3-66 4-70 5-82 6-107 7-367 8-399 9-431 10-537

2nd Inns: 1-10 2-22 3-92

Bonus Points - Sussex 5, Middx 3

Bowling	Ovs	Md	R	Wk	wd	nb	Ovs	Md	R	Wk	wd	nb
Dawes	35	2	126	3	3	0	7	3	25	2	0	0
Keegan	32.2	4	120	4	0	0	7	2	29	0	0	0
Cook	30	7	83	1	0	1	2	0	9	0	0	0
Peploe	28	2	100	0	4	1	6	2	20	0	0	0
Weekes	27	3	101	2	0	0	5.5	0	23	1	0	0

MIDDLESEX

#	Batsman	1st Innings		2nd Innings	
1	A.J. Strauss *	c: Prior b: Martin-Jenkins	138	c: Ambrose b: Lewry	4
2	S.G. Koenig	b: Lewry	5	Lbw b: Martin-Jenkins	16
3	O.A. Shah	(4) Lbw b: Mushtaq	140	st: Ambrose b: Davis	34
4	B.J. Hutton	(3) Lbw b: Lewry	1	(3) c: Martin-Jenkins b: Taylor	36
5	E.C. Joyce	Lbw b: Mushtaq	22	b: Mushtaq	31
6	P.N. Weekes	c: Ambrose b: Mushtaq	31	c: Prior b: Mushtaq	65
7	D.C. Nash +	c: Adams b: Mushtaq	15	(8) b: Lewry	5
8	S.J. Cook	b: Davis	11	(9) b: Mushtaq	11
9	C. Peploe	not out	0	(7) Lbw b: Lewry	13
10	C.B. Keegan	c: Adams b: Mushtaq	3		3
11	J.H. Dawes	c: Prior b: Mushtaq	0	Lbw b: Mushtaq	2
12					

	1st Innings			2nd Innings		
Extras	b 7	lb 13	wd 0	nb 6	Extras	26
Extras	b 11	lb 11	wd 0	nb 8	Extras	30
Overs	100		Provisional Total	392		
Overs	96.2		Provisional Total	250		
Pens	0	Wkts	10	Total	392	
Pens	0	Wkts	10	Total	250	

Fall of wickets 1st Inns: 1-17 2-33 3-252 4-309 5-334 6-374 7-387 8-387 9-390 10-392

2nd Inns: 1-4 2-42 3-79 4-124 5-152 6-201 7-215 8-241 9-244 10-250

Bonus Points - Middx 4, Sussex 3

Bowling	Ovs	Md	R	Wk	wd	nb	Ovs	Md	R	Wk	wd	nb
Lewry	20	6	53	2	0	0	25	8	73	3	0	0
Taylor	15	2	66	0	0	3	10	1	30	1	0	4
Mushtaq Ahmed	40	4	145	6	0	0	35.2	8	80	4	0	0
Martin-Jenkins	14	2	46	1	0	0	7	3	12	1	0	0
Davis	11	0	62	1	0	0	19	4	33	1	0	0

SUSSEX WON BY 7 WICKETS

Opposite Mark Davis, with 168 against Middlesex, consolidated the recovery that Prior had begun.

SUSSEX v. LANCASHIRE AT OLD TRAFFORD
Wednesday to Saturday, 10 to 13 September 2003

Playing Lancashire at Old Trafford was always going to be a tall order, even though Sussex were riding high after successive convincing wins in their last three matches. The northerners remained the only club with a realistic chance of denying Sussex the Championship and, sadly, the County suffered a dreadful attack of stage fright when they travelled north.

The first morning of the match was enveloped in Manchester drizzle and, in some respects, this ought to have been to Sussex's advantage. A draw would have helped them close in on the ten points they needed for the Championship. When play got under way Lancashire, who had won the toss, lost Mark Chilton to an excellent diving catch by Tim Ambrose off the bowling of Billy Taylor and, with the score on 66, Iain Sutcliffe flicked Jason Lewry nonchalantly off his legs to be brilliantly caught by Mark Davis at square leg. Although Mushtaq, brought on in the 21st over, provided his usual fare of leg and top-spinners together with some googlies and appealed with his usual gusto, Mal Loye and Stuart Law added an unbroken 159 so that, at the close with 68 overs gone, Lancashire were on 225 for two. It had been a contest between the leading run-scorer and the leading wicket-taker of the season and Law had won it with some ease.

The weather was not significantly better on the second day and only 43 overs were possible. Loye and Law took their 3rd-wicket partnership to 241 before the former top-edged Robin Martin-Jenkins to end the highest of his five first-class centuries in the season. Law, now joined by Carl Hooper, spurned an offer of the light 35 minutes before the close and, when Taylor started to pitch short, words were exchanged, most regrettably, between the Australian and the bowler. Although Hooper and Chris Schofield were both dismissed before the close, Lancashire had moved to 368 for five and a draw seemed at this stage to be the most likely result.

Warren Hegg, Lancashire's captain, decided to inflict more pain on the Sussex attack on the Friday morning and did not declare until his side's total had reached 450 for six, with Law unbeaten on 163 and Mushtaq still waiting for his 100th wicket of the season. Sussex needed 301 to avoid the follow-on and, despite the early loss of Richard Montgomerie, Murray Goodwin and Tony Cottey took the score sensibly to 122 before the latter was out in mid-afternoon. His dismissal heralded a disastrous collapse as six wickets went down for 35 runs in 11 overs on a pitch that continued to play quite easily. Goodwin batted resolutely, but when he had made 87 he attempted to hook Peter Martin and suffered a deep cut on his right eyebrow. This held up play for about ten minutes while the physiotherapists from both sides administered dressings, but he then went on to his third hundred of the season which was sympathetically applauded by the crowd. In the meantime Mushtaq did much better with the bat than he had done with the ball and hammered a typically robust half-century before the innings subsided 50 runs short of its target. Goodwin was still undefeated and became the first Sussex

Opposite Murray Goodwin's gallant 118 was to no avail in
Sussex's catastrophic defeat against Lancashire at Old Trafford
in the middle of September.

batsman to play through a completed innings since Bill Athey had achieved this feat against Kent in 1994.

Having watched wrist-spinner Mushtaq dismantle side after side throughout the summer, Sussex were themselves undone by something different – the finger spin of slow left-armer Gary Keedy, who bowled line and length and took five wickets. Apparently he quite enjoyed showing up Pakistani spinners, as he had taken seven wickets in the match against Surrey in August when Saqlain had, like Mushtaq in this match, been wicketless. Hegg had no compunction, of course, in sending Sussex in again and Montgomerie failed once more, while nightwatchman Taylor was also dismissed before the close when Sussex were on 21 for two, with Chris Adams, who had come in first in place of the injured Goodwin, still there on 19 not out.

By the final morning, the pitch had started to deteriorate and the ball was turning, albeit slowly, but also keeping low. Adams and Cottey batted with reasonable ease until Adams holed out at point with the score on 61. Ambrose's prompt dismissal brought in Goodwin, now with seven stitches in his head wound, at number 6. Cottey had been using his feet well to Keedy, but when he tried to sweep – never the best expedient on a slow wicket – he got an under-edge on to his pad and was caught in the leg trap. Martin-Jenkins faced some 45 balls without really middling anything until Martin uprooted his stumps and, soon after lunch, there were only Prior, Davis and Mushtaq to help Goodwin try to avoid the innings defeat. They were singularly unsuccessful and when Goodwin, well forward to Keedy, was adjudged lbw for 57 and eighth man out, the end was close. At 3.20 p.m. Sussex went down by an innings, as Keedy added a further five wickets to end the match with a ten-wicket haul.

Sussex had come to the match needing ten points to secure the Championship. In the end, probably by dint of looking for points rather than playing in the positive manner which they had adopted all season, they went away with only four. Chris Adams, talking to The Argus after the game, remained upbeat: 'We've played good cricket all year and we will make sure that we get it right for the last game and enjoy the moment.'

Lancashire (22 points) beat Sussex (4 points) by an innings and 19 runs.

Opposite Murray Goodwin returns to the pavilion with his head bandaged after having misjudged a hook off Peter Martin.

LANCASHIRE v SUSSEX
at Old Trafford
on Wed. 10th, Thurs .11th, Fri. 12th, Sat. 13th September 2003

Toss won by: Lancashire – elected to bat
Umpires: J. W. Lloyds
A. G. T. Whitehead

Scorers: A. West
J. F. Hartridge

LANCASHIRE	FIRST INNINGS		SECOND INNINGS
1	M. J. Chilton(21)...... .. ct. Ambrose ... b. Taylor	6	....
2	I. J. Sutcliffe(5)......ct. Davis ......b. Lewry ...	38	....
3	M. B. Loye(1)... ct. Montgomerie b. M-Jenkins	144	....
4	S. G. Law(2)....................Not Out	163	....
5	C. L. Hooper(17)...... l.b.w. ....b. Lewry	33	....
6	G. Chapple(3)...........................b. Lewry	14	....
7	W. K. Hegg*+(10)....................Not Out	26	....
8	C. P. Schofield(15)........................b. Taylor	1	....
9	P. J. Martin(24)		....
10	G. Keedy(23)..		....
11	J. Wood(7)..		....
	Extras b- 4 lb- 12 w- 1 nb- 8	25	Extras b- lb- w- nb-

										TOTAL	(for 6 dec)	450	TOTAL								

Fall of   1   2   3   4   5   6   7   8   9   1   2   3   4   5   6   7   8   9
Wickets   21   66 307 363 368 414

BOWLING ANALYSIS	O	M	R	W	WD	NB		O	M	R	W	WD	NB
Lewry	26.3	3	125	3	1			....	....	....	....	....	....
Taylor	35	8	114	2	....	4		....	....	....	....	....	....
Martin-Jenkins	23	7	73	1	....	....		....	....	....	....	....	....
Mushtaq	37	6	99	0	....	....		....	....	....	....	....	....
Davis	5	1	23	0	....	....		....	....	....	....	....	....

SUSSEX	FIRST INNINGS		SECOND INNINGS	
1.	R. R. Montgomerie(7)...... l.b.w. .... b. Keedy	10	.........l.b.w. .... b. Martin ...	2
2.	M. W. Goodwin(3).......................... Not Out	118	.........l.b.w............b. Keedy..........	57
3.	P. A. Cottey(2).............. ct. Chapple b. Wood	40	.........ct. Sub...........b. Keedy..........	32
4.	C. J. Adams(1)*.............. ct. Chapple b. Wood	1	.........ct. Law...........b. Wood..........	35
5.	T. R. Ambrose(11)+........................b. Wood	0	.........ct. Suttcliffe....b. Wood..........	2
6.	R. S. C. Martin-Jenkins(12).. ct. Hegg ...b. Keedy	2	.........................b. Martin..........	6
7.	M. J. Prior(13)................ ct. Law .... b. Keedy	2	.........ct. Schofield....b. Keedy..........	10
8.	M. J. G. Davis(8)............ ct. Law .... b. Keedy	2	.........ct. Suttcliffe....b. Keedy..........	11
9.	Mushtaq Ahmed(9)...........ct. Chilton . b. Hooper ...	54	.........................ct & b. Schofield....	16
10.	J. D. Lewry(5)........................... b. Hooper ...	2	.........................not out............	7
11.	B. V. Taylor(22).............. ct. Schofield b. Keedy ...	0	.........l.b.w. .... b. Keedy	0
12.	M. H. Yardy(20)			
	Extras b- 9 lb- 3 w- nb- 8	20	Extras b- 0 lb- 2 w- 0 nb- 0	2

								TOTAL	(all out)	251	TOTAL	(all out)						180

Fall of   1   2   3   4   5   6   7   8   9   1   2   3   4   5   6   7   8   9
Wickets   28 122 126 126 143 147 157 238 240   20   21   61   67   73   96 125 146 164

BOWLING ANALYSIS	O	M	R	W	WD	NB		O	M	R	W	WD	NB
Martin	15	4	40	0	....	2		20	7	43	2	....	....
Chapple	15	2	54	0	....	....							
Keedy	28	5	106	5	....	....		32	6	61	5	....	....
Wood	9	3	17	3	....	2		14	4	27	2	....	....
Hooper	5	0	17	2	....	....		17	3	33		....	....
Schofield	1	0	5	0	....	....		4	....	14	1	....	....

Lancashire won by an innings and 19 runs   Lancashire 22 pts   Sussex 4 pts

Spectators are reminded that any racially abusive comments and actions will result in ejection from the ground and possible further action.

SCORING OF POINTS

(a) For a win, 14 points, plus any points scored in the first innings.

(b) In a tie, each side to score seven points plus any points scored in the first innings.

(c) In a drawn match, each side to score four points plus any points scored in the first innings.

(d) If the scores are equal in a drawn match the side batting in the fourth innings to score seven points, plus any points scored in the first innings, and the opposing side to score four points plus any points scored in the first innings.

(e) **First Innings Points**
(awarded only for performance in **the first 130 overs** of each 1st innings retained whatever the result of the match)

(i) A maximum of five batting points to be available as under:
200 to 249 runs - 1 point
250 to 299 runs - 2 points
300 to 349 runs - 3 points
350 to 399 runs - 4 points
400 runs or over - 5 points

(ii) A maximum of three bowling points to be available as under
3 to 5 wickets taken - 1 point
6 to 8 wickets taken - 2 points
9 to 10 wickets taken - 3 points

(iii) If penalty runs are awarded to a team which at that time has faced less than 130 overs in their 1st innings, those penalty runs will be considered as counting towards the total as far as the award of bonus points is concerned.

(f) If play starts when less than eight hours playing time remains and a one innings match is played, no first innings points shall be scored. The side winning on the one innings to score 14 points. In a tie, each side to score seven points. In a drawn match, each side to score four points.

CHAMPIONSHIP OVER-RATE PENALTIES

The minimum over-rate to be achieved by counties will be 16 overs per hour. Overs will be calculated at the end of the match and penalties applied on a match-by-match basis.
For each over (fractions to be ignored) that a side has bowled short of the target number, 0.25 points will be deducted as follows:
1 over short: 0.25 points deducted
2 overs short: 0.50 points deducted
3 overs short: 0.75 points deducted
etc.

HOURS OF PLAY†

1st, 2nd and 3rd days:
11.00 a.m. - 6.30 p.m. (min. 104 overs)
4th day:
11.00 a.m. - 6.00 p.m. (min. 80 overs plus 16 overs)

INTERVALS†

1st, 2nd and 3rd days:
Lunch 1.15pm, Tea 4.10pm or when 32 overs remain to be bowled, whichever is the later.
4th day:
Lunch 1.00pm. Tea 3.40pm.

†September matches commence at 10.30am.

NEW BALL AVAILABLE AFTER 90 OVERS
* Captain   † Wicket Keeper

Opposite Billy Taylor appeals enthusiastically against a Lancashire batsman at Old Trafford.

Sussex came to their last match of the season – with Leicestershire at Hove – needing six bonus points to take them out of the reach of Lancashire and to secure the County Championship for the first time in their history. They had endured a serious blip at Old Trafford where Lancashire had inflicted an innings defeat on them, but their team spirit had not been blunted and there was every feeling that, in the fine September weather, they would have every chance of securing the points from Leicestershire, one of the lower-placed counties.

Phillip DeFreitas won the toss for the visitors and decided to bat on what looked to be a Hove 'belter'. John Maunders and Darren Maddy made a confident start against Jason Lewry from the Sea End and Billy Taylor coming down the slope from the Cromwell Road End. Forty-two runs were on the board before Maunders, in attempting to pull Robin Martin-Jenkins, who had come on as first change, skied an easy catch to mid-on. This brought in the Australian overseas player Brad Hodge, the scorer of a massive 302 against Nottinghamshire at Trent Bridge just over three weeks previously. The 2nd-wicket pair seemed on top of their game, but Chris Adams soon brought on Mushtaq to occupy the Sea End while he alternated his seamers at the other end. It looked as though Leicestershire would hold out until lunch, but with the last ball before the interval Mushtaq bowled Hodge and, in doing so, reached his 100 wickets for the season. 'A lifetime's ambition', Mushtaq claimed, remembering that an injury had probably precluded his doing so eight years previously when he had been with Somerset. It was, of course, more than a minor milestone, as the last bowler to reach the 100 mark in the Championship was Somerset's Andrew Caddick in 1998 and the last spinner to do so was Northamptonshire's Anil Kumble as far back as 1995, coincidentally the year when Mushtaq had just failed.

After the lunch interval Mushtaq, the Sussex fox, was soon among the Leicestershire chickens, getting John Sadler stumped and Luke Wright caught, both for ducks, while Billy Taylor had Maddy picked up at backward point and Paul Nixon caught behind. DeFreitas never gives up without a fight, but his well-struck 23 was not enough to put any respectability into his side's total. Sussex, with three bowling points, were halfway towards their goal. When the Sussex innings began Richard Montgomerie was soon caught behind, but Murray Goodwin and Tony Cottey guided the County to 137 for one at the close, when they needed another 163 runs for the title.

The Thursday morning dawned both expectantly and cautiously. Matches late in the season start at 10.30 a.m. and initially there was some cloud cover before the sun eventually began to break through. Umpire Mervyn Kitchen was held up by traffic on the A27 and the former Sussex batsman and now a respected coach Les Lenham officiated at square leg for the first 35 minutes of the day. The Leicestershire quick bowlers clearly found the conditions to their advantage and Goodwin and Cottey went on with extreme caution. Only 18 runs were scored in the first hour and Cottey was caught behind not long after reaching his 50. The second hour saw a decided increase in the tempo as skipper Chris Adams joined Goodwin and by the time lunch came at 12.45 p.m., after two-and-a-quarter hours' cricket, the score had moved on to 285 for two, still 15 runs short of the magical figure.

Above Mushtaq bowls Leicestershire's Australian batsman Brad Hodge to record his 100th wicket of the season on the opening day of the final match of the season at Hove in middle to late September.
Below Mushtaq shows his delight at capturing 100 wickets.

Above Mushtaq's team-mates congratulate him on his achievement. *Below* Tim Ambrose stumps Leicestershire batsman John Sadler for a duck off Mushtaq's bowling as Tony Cottey looks on at Hove.

Play resumed at 1.25 p.m. and, after 18 minutes' further cricket, Goodwin pulled a short ball from DeFreitas to the mid-wicket boundary close to the pavilion and the scoreboard moved from 298 to 302. Sussex had won the Championship! The spectators rose and applauded, Adams rushed down the pitch to hug Goodwin, the loudspeakers came forth with 'Sussex by the Sea' and the Sussex players streamed out of their new pavilion to engage in a victory parade around the ground. For many of the unusually large crowd which filled the ground this was a moment to savour, with misty eyes perhaps, but certainly to savour. For many Sussex members – a preponderance of county aficionados doubtless belong to the older generation – this was something which few can have dared to hope for, especially after the lean years of Sussex cricket. But it was all real and just how they enjoyed it!

The umpires and Leicestershire skipper Phillip DeFreitas had apparently agreed in advance that, when the great moment came, they would be happy to allow a break in proceedings and ten minutes elapsed before Goodwin and Adams went on. Goodwin, whose hundred had come with a powerful back-foot drive, reached his 150 in a further 36 balls and moved towards his double ton, while Adams struck powerfully off his legs and straight down the ground. With his score on 86 the Sussex skipper twice reverse-swept the ultra-slow off-spin of Jeremy Snape for four and then struck him straight for six to reach his 100. When he left, caught at long on, Ambrose came in to partner Goodwin. The crowd must have been wondering for how long the ferocious onslaught would go on, yet the Leicestershire out-cricket remained reasonably focused. The bowling, it is true, was just a little short of Test class, but the fielding held up well and few runs were gifted to the opposition. Goodwin reached his 250 and people in the crowd wondered whether he would be allowed to go on to 300. He certainly was, and soon afterwards he made his solitary error when, having reached 304, he pulled Wright in the air towards the pavilion and Sadler, at mid-wicket, fluffed the catch. Voices then started to inquire: 'Who has made the highest score for Sussex?' Sundry replies came forth: 'It must be Ranjitsinhji', 'No, it was surely C.B. Fry' or 'What about Alan Wells? He made a packet against Yorkshire not so long ago.' The *cognoscenti* knew, of course. It was Duleepsinhji, who early in the 1930 season took 333 off Northamptonshire on the very same Hove ground.

This was Sussex's golden day and it was axiomatic that Goodwin would break the record. When Ambrose was caught for 82 the closure was applied on 614 for four at a run-rate of 4.87 per over – the third time Sussex had passed 600 in the season – and a beaming Goodwin walked back to the pavilion with an unbeaten 335 to his name, having faced 390 balls in 489 minutes of batting and having hit 52 fours and a six. What was perhaps forgotten in the euphoria of the day was that he had scored 264 runs in less than a full day's play!

Leicestershire had a mountain to climb and, with the loss before the close of Maunders and Snape, who was substituting for Maddy who had fallen sick, things did not appear to be going their way.

The Sussex team had celebrated well, perhaps too well, on the Thursday night and, when the side took the field on the Friday morning minus the injured Mushtaq, they were more than a little below par. David Masters, recruited as a bowler from Kent in the close season, had been sent in the previous evening as nightwatchman and, although another of

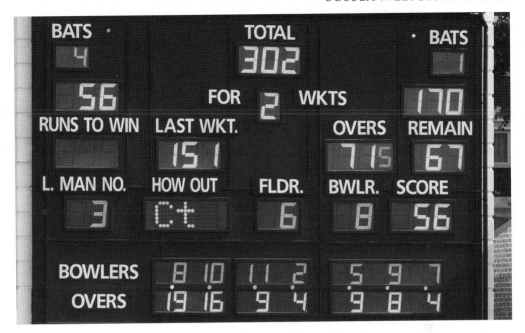

BATS ·		TOTAL			· BATS	
4		302			1	
56		FOR	2	WKTS	170	
RUNS TO WIN	LAST WKT.			OVERS	REMAIN	
	151			715	67	
L. MAN NO.	HOW OUT		FLDR.	BWLR.	SCORE	
3	Ct		6	8	56	
BOWLERS	8	10	11	2	5	9	7
OVERS	19	16	9	4	9	8	4

Above The Hove scoreboard shows the 300 score. The Championship has been won!

Opposite Chris Adams drives to mid-wicket on the way to his hundred against Leicestershire.

the same ilk, George Walker, went quite quickly and Lewry dismissed the dangerous Hodge, Masters continued to bat in fine style. For much of this time Adams was also missing from the field and Sussex were captained by the substitute, their vice-captain, James Kirtley – a rare occurrence in the county game. Joined by Sadler on 69 for four, Masters went past his best previous score of 68 in 2002 and completed his hundred before falling to a reckless shot with the score on 277 for five. Sadler, too, batted well and completed his second first-class hundred in only ten innings, but when Lewry had the now-recovered Maddy lbw for 29 the floodgates opened. 353 for five rapidly became 380 all out. Lewry, bowling with hostility from the Sea End, took all the last five wickets and ended with a career-best eight for 106 as Sussex ran out winners by an innings.

That marked the end of the match, but it was not the end of the day. Fireworks exploded from the Gilligan Stand and the large crowd massed in front of the players' balcony as John Carr, the ECB director of cricket, presented to Chris Adams the Championship pennant, the Lord's Taverners gold trophy and Frizzell's cheque for £105,000. Carr added to the general mood of fun by congratulating 'Surrey – sorry, Sussex' on winning the Championship and there followed a host of regulation speeches, not always audible to the crowd below, before people happily drifted away from this unique day. It is difficult to believe that Hove will ever see its like again.

Sussex (22 points) beat Leicestershire (1 point) by an innings and 55 runs.

Opposite Murray Goodwin celebrates reaching his 200.

Above A joyful crowd applauds as Sussex clinch the Championship.

Right Mark Davis and Mushtaq cavort across the ground at Hove as the game is held up for celebrations for Sussex's winning the Championship.

Far right Murray Goodwin returns to the pavilion after having scored 335 not out from Sussex's 614 for four declared against Leicestershire – the highest individual score by a Sussex batsman, which beat Duleepsinhji's 333 against Northamptonshire in 1930.

SUSSEX v LEICESTERSHIRE

at Hove on 17th - 20th September - Frizzell County Championship Division 1

Leics won the toss and elected to bat

SUSSEX WON BY AN INNINGS & 55 RUNS

SUSSEX — 1st Innings

#	Batsman		Runs
1	M.W. Goodwin [3]	not out	335
2	R.R. Montgomerie [7]	c: Nixon b: DeFreitas	10
3	P.A. Cottey [2]	c: Nixon b: DeFreitas	56
4	C.J. Adams * [1]	c: Drakes b: Walker	102
5	T.R. Ambrose + [11]	c: Sadler b: Hodge	82
6	R.S.C. Martin-Jenkins [12]		
7	M.J. Prior [13]		
8	M.J.G. Davis [8]		
9	Mushtaq Ahmed [9]		
10	J.D. Lewry [5]		
11	B.V. Taylor [22]		
12	M.H. Yardy [20]		

b 12	lb 9	wd 0	nb 8	Extras	29
Overs	126			Provisional Total	614
Pens	0		Wkts	4 decl	Total	614

Fall of 1st Inns: 1 - 24 2 -151 3 -418 4 -614
wickets

Bowling

Bowling	Ovs	Md	R	Wk	wd	nb
DeFreitas	28	4	94	2	0	2
Drakes	19	2	64	0	0	0
Masters	18	0	88	0	0	1
Maddy	4	0	21	0	0	0
Wright	19	0	95	0	0	0
Snape	12	0	72	0	0	1
Walker	19	1	92	1	0	0
Hodge	6	0	51	1	0	0
Maunders	1	0	16	0	0	0

LEICS

#	Batsman	1st Innings	Runs	2nd Innings	Runs
1	J.K. Maunders	c: Lewry b: Martin-Jenkins	21	c: Martin-Jenkins b: Lewry	15
2	D.L. Maddy	c: Cottey b: Taylor	55	(7) Lbw b: Lewry	29
3	B.J. Hodge	b: Mushtaq	36	(5) c: Ambrose b: Lewry	1
4	J.L. Sadler	st: Ambrose b: Mushtaq	0	(6) b: Lewry	145
5	L.J. Wright	(6) c: Montgomerie b: Mushtaq	0	(9) not out	11
6	P.A. Nixon +	(5) c: Ambrose b: Taylor	1	(8) c: Goodwin b: Lewry	0
7	G.W. Walker	(10) not out	4	(4) c: sub (Hopkinson) b: Lewry	21
8	P.A.J. DeFreitas *	(8) b: Martin-Jenkins	23	(10) b: Lewry	0
9	J.N. Snape	(7) c: Ambrose b: Lewry	13	(2) c: Adams b: Taylor	1
10	V.C. Drakes	(9) c: Ambrose b: Martin-Jenkins	8	(11) c: Ambrose b: Lewry	0
11	D.D. Masters	b: Mushtaq	2	(3) c: Martin-Jenkins b: Taylor	119
12					

b 5	lb 6	wd 1	nb 4	Extras	16	b	lb	wd	nb	Extras	38
Overs	69.5			Provisional Total	179	Overs	88.1			Provisional Total	380
Pens	0		Wkts	10	Total	179	Pens	0	Wkts	10	Total	380

Fall of 1st Inns: 1 - 42 2 -111 3 -117 4 -117 5 - 118 6 -118 7 -142 8 -167 9 -174 10-179
wickets 2nd Inns: 1 - 16 2 - 20 3 - 65 4 - 69 5 -227 6 - 353 7 - 353 8 - 370 9 - 370 10-380

Bowling

Bowling	Ovs	Md	R	Wk	wd	nb	Ovs	Md	R	Wk	wd	nb
Lewry	15	4	37	1	0	0	24.1	3	106	8	0	0
Taylor	18	6	40	2	1	2	21.2	6	84	2	0	8
Martin-Jenkins	12	6	20	3	0	0	9.4	0	60	0	0	0
Mushtaq Ahmed	24.5	3	71	4	0	0	-	-	-	-	-	-
Davis	-	-	-	-	-	-	25	9	75	0	0	0
Cottey	-	-	-	-	-	-	4	0	15	0	0	0
Goodwin	-	-	-	-	-	-	3	0	17	0	0	0
Adams	-	-	-	-	-	-	1	0	1	0	0	0

UMPIRES :
T.E. Jesty
M.J. Kitchen
SCORERS :
J.F. Hartridge
G. York

HOURS OF PLAY
Days 1 - 3: 10.30am - 6pm
Day 4 : 10.30am - 5.30pm
Lunch
Days 1 - 3: 12.45pm - 1.25pm
Day 4 : 12.30pm - 1.10pm
Tea
Days 1 - 3 : 3.40pm - 4pm
or when 32 overs remain to
be bowled, whichever is later
Day 4 : 3.10pm - 3.30pm

1st Inns Bonus Pts
(Only in the first 130 Overs)
Batting (Max 5pts)
1pt at achieving 200, 250,
300, 350 and 400 runs.
Bowling (Max 3pts)
1 pt for taking 3, 6 & 9 wkts

Opposite above The sun-drenched scene at Hove from the last match of a 'glorious summer' for Sussex.

Opposite below The final rites. Leicestershire's last pair, Luke Wright and Vasbert Drakes, walk off as Sussex, the new county Champions, record their tenth win of the season by defeating the Midland county by an innings and 55 runs.

CELEBRATIONS AT HOVE

Left The men behind the scenes: Keith Greenfield (academy director), Mark Robinson (First XI coach) and Peter Moores (director of cricket) savour success.

Above The guiding hands: captain Chris Adams and director of cricket Peter Moores.

Below A contented team. From left to right: Tim Ambrose, Matt Prior, Murray Goodwin, Tony Cottey, Kevin Innes, Mushtaq Ahmed (in front), Chris Adams, Mark Davis, Richard Montgomerie, Michael Yardy.

Opposite The smile of Sussex captain Chris Adams tells the whole story.

Above The team show off the Championship pennant. From left to right: Kevin Innes, Matt Prior, Tim Ambrose, Chris Adams, Shaun Rashid, Richard Montgomerie, Jason Lewry, Tony Cottey.

Below A bibulous but happy group: Tim Ambrose, Jason Lewry, Tony Cottey, Kevin Innes, Murray Goodwin and Mark Davis celebrate.

Opposite John Barclay, Sussex captain in 1981 – the last occasion when Sussex came close to the Championship – handles the silverware.

Above The Sussex member to whom Tony Pigott promised success before the member died was there to see Sussex win.

Opposite above The Sussex captain celebrates with some members.

Opposite below The trophy is held aloft on the balcony of the players' pavilion.

Words And Thoughts

CHRIS ADAMS (captain of Sussex CCC): 'It has been a long journey for the past six years and we have worked very hard for it. The club has never won the Championship before and a lot of the core membership have been coming here for years. We have given them some good times before, but I am sure every one of them will remember this day and treasure it for ever.'

THE TIMES: 'Sussexing Up: Play up, play up and play the game for pleasure.'

THE DAILY TELEGRAPH: 'Sussex's long wait: To belong to a cricket club that was formed in 1839 and since tried unsuccessfully for 113 years to win the County Championship is a severe test of loyalty. Long overdue congratulations, therefore, to the supporters of Sussex County Cricket Club, who yesterday saw their team become Champions for the first time. A salute from all who love the game to Sussex's faithful followers.'

FRANK KEATING (The Guardian): 'Joy unconfined as Sussex top the table.' Champagne shaken and sprayed at seventh-heaven Hove... beer and high spirits at more raffish Brighton... and cheers and church bells at each and every place the world over where expats cup an ear to the close-of-play scoreboard. Sussex are county Champions not so much at last as at long, long last.'

DAVID GILBERT (chief executive at Cricket New South Wales and chief executive of Sussex CCC 1999-2001): 'Congratulations on a truly memorable and historic achievement. Enjoy the celebrations!'

TED DEXTER (Sussex CCC 1957-68 and captain 1960-65): 'Absolutely thrilled. Little Mush has made a huge difference but it is a good all-round side. When the big names fail somebody chips in.'

TONY GREIG (Sussex CCC 1966-78 and captain 1973-78): 'Congratulations to all at Sussex! I am proudly wearing my Sussex cuffs and tie on this great day.'

JOHN BARCLAY (Sussex CCC 1970-86 and captain 1981-86): 'We are not used to this sort of thing and, frankly, it comes as something of a surprise.'

ALAN WELLS (Sussex CCC 1981-96 and captain 1992-96): 'A fantastic team effort.'

TONY PIGOTT (Sussex CCC 1978-93 and chief executive 1997-99): 'One part of the vision was to win the Championship in five years. At the time, people thought I was completely mad. This is the sixth year – so I was one out.'

THE SUSSEX CRICKET SOCIETY: 'Please convey to all members concerned the Society's congratulations on winning the Championship. It is a tremendous achievement. The winning hit will be remembered for a very long time.'

SURREY CCC: 'Warm congratulations to you for your magnificent achievement in winning the Championship for the first time in your history.'

PETER MOORES (director of cricket): 'Next season will be a new challenge. Surrey will want their title back, Lancashire will be strong and everyone starts with a clean sheet. 'Success promotes belief and, until you win, you never really know that what you are doing is right. There is still so much room for improvement here, and winning makes you want to get better. It's very exciting.'

ANALYSIS
Why Sussex won the Championship

'Anything before the Championship will be known as Sussex B.C.'
Paul Weaver *(The Guardian)*

Finding facts to fit reasons or, conversely, reasons to fit facts, is no easy task. The facts are that Sussex won the County Championship in 2003, but the reasons will be debated for many a long evening as memories of Goodwin's pull to mid-wicket are mulled over throughout the bars and sitting rooms of Sussex. At the outset some did not rate their chances at all. Rob Steen and Bob Woolmer, assessing 'The good, the bad and the middling' in the May edition of the *Wisden Cricket Monthly* took the bleak view that Sussex 'won't win much but will improve', while at the same time predicting that they would move from 6th place in 2002 to 9th place in the 2003 Championship. Forecasting sport is a hard task, especially for the professionals.

Despite the seven, or perhaps eight, occasions when Sussex reached second place in the County Championship only the most recent attempt – in 1981 under John Barclay's leadership – had actually come close to the title. In fact, many have suggested that they were distinctly unlucky at that time as they had two matches washed out and umpire Peter Stevens rejected what many saw as a plumb lbw against the last man in the match with Nottinghamshire – the county who did, in fact, lift the trophy. As Barclay chivalrously said at the time: 'We'll win it one day and, when we do, the joy will be unconfined, you see.' We did and it was – he was right.

From the time of the near miss in 1981 the record of Sussex in the Championship was undistinguished. Between 1982 and 1996 Sussex's average position was just over 11th – only Glamorgan had a worse record, while Somerset were on a par with Sussex and Durham had joined only in 1992 – so it was perhaps unsurprising that eventually there were ructions among the members. The AGM in the spring of 1997 unseated the committee and a new regime was installed. The previous committee, headed by Alan Caffyn and not unlike many a similar body up and down the land, had perhaps treated Sussex CCC as a personal fiefdom and had been less proactive than they might have been in advancing the aims of the club. The new regime was headed by Robin Marlar as chairman and Tony Pigott as chief executive. Both had been Sussex players, Marlar from 1951 to 1968, with a largely successful period as captain between 1955 and 1959, and Pigott from 1978 to 1993 when he was not retained after taking only 20 wickets at an average of over 40 and ostensibly bowling poorly in the 1993 NatWest final which Sussex lost off the very last ball.

Pigott set out aggressively to put matters right and was interested only in players who were prepared to 'run through brick walls for Sussex'. Certainly, and predictably, it did not pay off immediately, as the team, bereft of six capped players including their captain Alan Wells, their best spinner Ian Salisbury, and an exciting wicketkeeper-batsman Martin Speight, ended up bottom of the Championship. Peter Moores, entrusted with the captaincy at short notice, struggled manfully with an essentially weak side. The batting relied mainly on Neil Taylor, imported from Kent, and Bill Athey, who did not even finish the season, while Mark Robinson headed the rather insubstantial bowling. The season overall might best be noted as one of 'experience.'

Pigott had, however, a few tricks up his sleeve. Having unsuccessfully attempted to recruit Australian master-spinner Shane Warne to the South Coast, he ventured up the M1 and at a motorway service station met Chris Adams of Derbyshire, who had felt frustrated in his home county and was keen to be released from his contract. While Moores moved over to be player-coach in 1998, Adams was offered the captaincy on what *Wisden* described as a 'jumbo-sized' contract, while two other Australians joined the County's ranks. Michael Bevan, discarded by Australia as a Test batsman but very highly regarded in the one-day game, became the overseas player, while David Gilbert, an Australian Test bowler who had been coaching at The Oval for two years was offered the post of director of cricket and *de facto* deputy to Pigott.

It was here that the first seeds of success for 2003 were sown. Sussex, amazingly, moved from 18th to 7th place in the Championship and Pigott admitted that he could not have hoped for better. 'If someone had offered me at the end of 1997 that we would be seventh in the Championship the next year, I would have laughed,' he told *Wisden*. Things were starting to fall into place. Adams had led the side well; Bevan, when not on Australian duty, had batted magnificently; James Kirtley and Jason Lewry had teamed up as a potent opening attack and Robin Martin-Jenkins was showing the signs of developing into a successful all-rounder. For 1999 Richard Montgomerie, strangely surplus to requirements at Northampton, was recruited to open the batting, Tony Cottey was engaged from Glamorgan and Umer Rashid from Middlesex, while Tasmanian Michael Di Venuto, a shrewd signing which bore the hallmarks of Gilbert's know-how, came in for Bevan, who needed a break from cricket. Sadly for Pigott, who had, as it were, started the ball rolling, he had made the classic error of recruiting someone more able than himself as his deputy and was succeeded as chief executive by David Gilbert. At the end of the 1999 season, however, 7th place had not been maintained and Sussex's 11th place consigned them to the lower of the two new divisions of the Championship. The 2000 season saw Bevan return *vice* Di Venuto – not a wholly popular move according to some, but one dictated by the terms of a contract – and Sussex, after leading their group in August, fell like a stone to the bottom of Division Two, that is to say, under the old format, plumb bottom of the whole Championship. It looked as if the new arrangements had proved to be a false dawn.

Nothing could have been further from the truth. Gilbert and Adams knew that they needed to make the wheel turn full circle in 2001 and they did just that. The shrewdest acquisition was that of Murray Goodwin, the former Zimbabwe batsman, who had decided to leave the Test arena. Gilbert, however, was also looking to the future. Tim Ambrose, born in New South Wales but with an EU passport, and Matt Prior, a product of Brighton College, aged 18 and 20 respectively, were drafted into the side, while a further ECB-qualified recruit was Mark Davis from South Africa. A side that had now been largely refashioned played to its potential and comfortably topped Division Two of the Championship and was promoted for the 2002 season. Some supporters, rather prematurely, claimed a 'Championship'.

If the two-division Championship has meaning – and many acknowledge its advantages – the standard of cricket in the upper division ought to be higher. In 2002 the Sussex side played well, but the success of the previous year was, predictably, not replicated. For all that, however, Sussex retained their position in Division One, albeit in 6th place, and their maturing side was well placed to achieve the great success of 2003.

At the end of 2001, David Gilbert, who had spent four years at Hove, was offered the post of chief executive with Cricket New South Wales and, after a period of interregnum, was succeeded in 2002 by Hugh Griffiths. Gilbert was a great loss to Sussex. Not only had he transformed the commercial and administrative side of the club, but his shrewd knowledge of the game, perhaps the product of his own experience as a Test player, had allowed him to recruit wisely. There was, however, one setback in the plans that he had laid, when the promising left-handed all-rounder Umer Rashid was drowned in April 2002, during the County's training expedition on the island of Grenada.

The side that took the field in 2003 bore no real resemblance to Sussex in 1997 and very little to the 1998 side. In 1997 Kirtley had played nine Championship matches and Martin-Jenkins two, while of the 1998 staff, the first year of the Adams captaincy, only the skipper, Kirtley, Martin-Jenkins and Lewry (who had missed the 1997 season through injury) remained. A weak and ineffective side had, in the course of seven seasons, been turned into Champions.

Leadership plays an important role, perhaps increasingly so, in sporting success. The acquisition of Chris Adams to lead Sussex can probably be seen as Pigott's greatest contribution to the Sussex renaissance, because his leadership has been central to success. Known as 'Grizzly' by his team, the now-thirty-three-year-old Adams is socially a friendly and amiable man, but on the field he is a powerful captain who seeks to dominate everything on which he sets his eyes. His aggressive and positive style of leadership – Sussex have tended to draw fewer matches than the average county – has paid dividends. It has perhaps brought the occasional brush with authority, especially when he meets up with like-minded people – Nasser Hussain is perhaps one – but that, in a sense, goes with the job. Under his captaincy Sussex have tended never to step back, but with his own team he has always had time to support players, such as Mushtaq, when the going got really tough.

One cannot, of course, lead a county side if one is a passenger in the playing sense, and Adams is certainly not that. Spectators, not only those with Sussex connections, have often remarked that, when he is batting in top form, cricket looks an entirely different game from that which has just preceded it. Despite an indifferent start to the season he came into form as July ran into August with a hundred in the Surrey match at Hove and, in the following game – against Lancashire, also at Hove – he made 330 runs in his two innings in over ten hours of batting, and dominated the scene. Sussex players subsequently commented that it was in this match that they knew that could win the Championship. In the course of his six seasons with Sussex he has made 5,819 Championship runs at an average of 40.13, scoring 16 hundreds and 27 fifties and taking some 115 catches. Into the bargain, he has taken the odd wicket when a stubborn partnership has needed to be broken. His own brilliant strokeplay brought him into international reckoning and, in the summer of 1998, he played two one-day internationals against South Africa and in the winter of 1999-2000 he was a member of the England touring party in South Africa where he played in all five Tests and in a further three one-day contests. Sussex fans certainly argue that he has not been given sufficient chances in the international sphere, even though they acknowledge his perceived weakness outside the off stump, but they believe that his temperament is such that it will stand him in good stead. After all, experts say that county cricket is 90 per cent ability and 10 per cent bottle, while at Test level this moves to 60 per cent ability and 40 per cent bottle.

If Adams was the frontman in Sussex's team, affairs off the field were largely in the hands of Peter Moores, the director of cricket. He came to Sussex in 1985 from Worcestershire to ply his trade as a wicketkeeper and useful batsman. Not immediately making the grade, he did not start to command a serious place in the side until two years later and only became first-choice 'keeper when Ian 'Gunner' Gould relinquished the gloves. At the beginning of the 1997 season he was asked by Tony Pigott to take the poisoned chalice, the captaincy of a weak and debilitated side. It was probably the worst job in cricket and there were many on the county circuit who both pitied and admired him. He stuck to his task with outstanding tenacity, but this did not prevent Sussex's ending up bottom of the Championship and, incidentally, of the AXA Life Sunday League. He knew that his was a stop-gap post and in the following year was happy to become player-coach and then, in the course of the next few years, coach, cricket manager/coach and Second XI captain and finally in 2003 director of cricket. At the end of 1997 he saw it as his duty, in consultation with the chief executive and the new captain, to seek to change the whole culture and environment at Hove. Moores aimed to create a strong work ethic in which players wanted to learn and improve their standards while enjoying what they were doing. In particular physical fitness and mental toughness were seen as central to their cricketing education.

So that the players were able to have the facilities to improve their standards the County set about a building programme at the Cromwell Road end of the Hove ground. They invested in high-quality outdoor nets and, although some older members were sad to see the George Cox Garden disappear, a new indoor school with a fine net complex and purpose-built players' changing accommodation was erected. Gradually a strong coaching team evolved – Moores himself, Mark Robinson, whose medium-pace bowling had been a linchpin of less happy seasons; Les Lenham, a Sussex opening bat of the 1950s and 1960s who had later become a distinguished national coach; Keith Greenfield, the academy director; and Craig Savage, a baseball coach whose task was to improve fielding, all came on stream. It was an impressive array. Moores himself also invested in a 'Crickstat' statistics system which has allowed him to record every ball during each summer. He has regarded attention to detail as vital to the production of good cricketers, who are able to watch their strengths and weaknesses on video, thus allowing the coach to deal with individual problems of attitude and technique. As Moores told Angus Fraser of *The Independent*: 'County cricket is changing and players are waking up. They do not just work, they work with a clear plan.'

Moores and Adams have been at the heart of Sussex's great success. The County must hope that they will continue together in harness. Adams believes that he has another five years of top cricket left in him, although the media talk of Moores as a possible successor to Duncan Fletcher as England manager/coach. He was a highly successful coach to the England 'A' side which toured the West Indies in the winter of 2000-2001 and his great success with Sussex makes such an appointment, however sad it might be for Sussex, eminently possible in the fullness of time.

The captain and director of cricket would not have achieved what they did without, of course, the self-belief and the ability of the players. Sussex were fortunate to possess in Murray Goodwin and Mushtaq Ahmed two overseas players who were not going to be required for Test duty with their respective countries. Goodwin had already retired from the international scene, while Mushtaq, despite believing that he had a rightful place with the Pakistan Test team, did not receive a call until September when the county season had ended. Goodwin – normally a number 3 batsman – played his last Test for Zimbabwe in 2000 and came on to the Sussex staff in 2001. Willingly accepting the role of an opening batsman since a vacancy occurred there, he has in his three seasons scored 4,196 Championship runs at an average of 53.11 with 15 hundreds and 13 fifties, including his last great innings of the 2003 season – 335 not out against Leicestershire.

Mushtaq Ahmed was, in the view of some Sussex supporters, an entirely different kettle of fish. Some thought that a Pakistani leg-spinner coming up to his thirty-third birthday in June might just be past his sell-by date. It was true that he had in 50 Tests for Pakistan taken 183 wickets (average 32.24) and in five seasons between 1993 and 1998 he had taken 281 Championship wickets (average 26.36) for Somerset, but his last year at Taunton had been a poor one as he had knee trouble – not the best thing for any bowler – as well as some domestic concerns. Since that time he had played 12 Tests for his country (the last in 2000), taken a mere 23 wickets (average 64.13) and seemed to have existed largely on the periphery of serious cricket. The Jeremiahs had got it completely wrong, although it is instructive to note that Sussex had sought to engage Harbhajan Singh and Stuart MacGill before finally plumping for Mushtaq. But he came to Sussex in fine fettle and soon set about plying his leg-spinners, frequently interspersed with almost as many 'flippers' and googlies. He bemused and bamboozled batsmen throughout Division One, appealing loudly and sometimes too frequently, and became the first bowler since 1998 to take 100 wickets in a Championship season and 114 in all matches. Some counties even started preparing pitches that they felt would not suit him, but it was a dry summer overall and he was not to be denied. Ten five-wicket innings hauls and five occasions where he took ten or more wickets in the match represented a quite stupendous effort and he was backed up by the side's out-cricket. One doubter even thought that Hampshire had been far wiser in recruiting Wasim Akram to their ranks. How dreadfully wrong he was proved to be, especially when Wasim fell ill and retired halfway through the season! It would be to ignore the obvious if one did not underline the fact that the 2003 summer was, for the most part, a dry one. When Shane Warne played for Hampshire in the relatively damp 2001 season he did well, but perhaps not quite as well as many hoped, or feared, depending upon their viewpoint. Had 2003 been just as damp, would Mushtaq have been quite as effective?

Sussex's close catching – Adams, Cottey, and Montgomerie in particular – was high class and it was found that Tim Ambrose behind the stumps read Mushtaq better than Matt Prior, who gracefully retired to the leg trap and took many useful catches. At the same time the rest of the fielding, despite the inevitable odd fall from grace, reached a high standard.

The great strength of the Sussex side in 2003 was its depth. If one part failed to function, another part did well. Initially, the top-order batting did not fulfil its potential except in the case of Tony Cottey. Goodwin's first 17 innings produced 496 runs (average 31.00) with three fifties, while his next 11 amassed exactly 1,000 runs (average 111.11). Montgomerie was a similar case: until the Surrey match at Hove he had played 19 innings, contributing a hundred at Horsham and two fifties, but his last six matches produced over 400 runs. This relative failure of the openers in the first half of the season was compensated by a number of factors. Cottey, whom many saw as being in the 'last-chance saloon' at the end of his five-year contract, ran into excellent form. Between the Warwickshire match at Edgbaston in early May and the Nottinghamshire game at Trent Bridge at the end of July he played 11 innings and failed to pass 50 in only two, and in five successive innings in the middle of this period he made 188 against Warwickshire at Hove, 107 and 98 against Essex at Arundel and 147 and 58 against Leicestershire at Leicester. Just as disappointing as the openers at the start of the season was Chris Adams himself. His first 17 innings produced a mere 318 runs with a top score of 62 against Kent at Tunbridge Wells, but there was something of 'cometh the hour, cometh the man' about his season and, when things became crucial, he took 107 off Surrey and then 140 and 190 off Lancashire, the only other teams who seriously challenged in the Championship race.

If, therefore, three of the top four showed some signs of fragility well into the middle part of the season, Tim Ambrose, Robin Martin-Jenkins and Matt Prior in the positions 5 to 7 batted particularly well. Ambrose did not score a hundred all season, but he contributed nine innings over fifty with 931 runs at an average of 40.47, while Martin-Jenkins had a splendid spell in early June when he scored half-centuries in four successive innings and top scored in three of them, while also recording his third first-class hundred. The most explosive of the three middle-order men was Prior. Ceding the keeper's gloves to Ambrose after the Kent game at Tunbridge Wells, he batted so well at times that many thought that he was too lowly placed at number 7. In the course of the season he made 1,006 Championship runs (average 47.90 and a strike rate of 74.96 runs per 100 balls) with four hundreds. His 133 at Horsham made mincemeat of Australian Test leg-spinner Stuart MacGill among others, while his 148 at Hove, when Sussex appeared to be collapsing against Middlesex, turned what could have been a disastrous defeat into an excellent win. Several others made useful contributions with the bat, not least Mushtaq, who contributed three fifties in his own adventurous style – his strike rate of 81.42 even exceeded Prior's – and Jason Lewry, who reached his first half-century in his ninth first-class season.

The bowling, of course, centred around Mushtaq, but several others also made their mark. James Kirtley just failed by one to reach the 50-wicket mark for the County, which he had achieved over the four previous seasons, but the reasons for this were clear. His usual opening partner, Jason Lewry, after a poor season during his benefit in 2002, was known to be concerned about the renewal of his contract, especially as Paul Hutchison, another left-arm pace bowler, had appeared in the Sussex ranks. His answer was to take 41 Championship wickets and see the Yorkshireman leave at the end of the season and move to Middlesex. Had the season been damper, the final place, that of the number 8 all-rounder, might have gone more often to Kevin Innes, but after his hundred at Horsham, scored wholly unusually from the twelfth-man slot (new ECB regulations allowed a player discarded from the England Test team to replace a previously nominated county player), he found that Mark Davis, with his off-spin, tended to get the selectors' nod over his own medium-pace. Davis is no Mushtaq, but his accurate bowling found a place in the attack and his batting, though not always consistent, blossomed incredibly in his 168 against Middlesex. A sadness at the end of the season was the fact that Billy Taylor decided to move back to his native Hampshire. At some points in the latter part of the season, when Kirtley was not playing, he proved to be the bowler who achieved the most.

Consistency of selection and, therefore, of team composition is an essential in most sports if success is to be achieved. Quite remarkably, the first seven places in the Sussex order (Montgomerie, Goodwin, Cottey, Adams, Ambrose, Martin-Jenkins, Prior) remained exactly the same for all sixteen Championship matches, except that Michael Yardy replaced Cottey at number 3 in the Surrey match at The Oval and Ambrose at number 5 in the Nottinghamshire match at Trent Bridge, while Mushtaq also occupied the number 9 slot throughout the season. The number 8 position was shared between Innes (six matches and one substitution for Kirtley) and Davis (ten matches), but the last two places enjoyed some variation. The preferred choice was, of course, the well-tried pair of Kirtley and Lewry, but injuries and Test calls meant that they missed five games each, the ten resulting slots being filled by Taylor (seven) and Hutchison (three, plus one substitution for Kirtley). It was clearly a great honour both to James Kirtley and to Sussex that he was required to play two Tests for England – and to do so well in the defeat of South Africa at Trent Bridge – but this achievement also had its downside. After the Fourth Test at Leeds Kirtley was found to be suffering from shin splints, which brought a premature end to his season, the second encounter with Surrey being his last appearance. What his absence in the last four Championship matches might have meant to Sussex's chances is, happily, only a matter of conjecture. In general, however, Sussex were fortunate that injuries did not seriously upset the balance of their side and, in fact, only fifteen players were called upon. The reserves, when Test calls and injuries made their appearance necessary, were in every case, except perhaps one, wholly equal to the task.

Sussex were clearly a stronger side at home than away, their average first-innings score on home soil amounting to 458. Of their ten victories seven were at home, five at Hove and one each at Horsham and Arundel – in fact, they did not lose at all when playing in Sussex. Their four losses away were all, strangely, on Test match grounds at Lord's, Edgbaston, Old Trafford and The Oval.

So what does lead to success? Long-term preparation, dedication, leadership, self-belief and team spirit, physical fitness, good training facilities, making the right selections – all these things were achieved by Sussex in 2003. Good fortune also plays its part in any success story, but it would be wrong to suggest that Sussex's great Championship in the glorious summer of 2003 was, in any way, achieved by chance.

FINAL COUNTY CHAMPIONSHIP TABLE
2003 - DIVISION ONE

	P	W	L	D	Bat	Bowl	Ded	Points
Sussex	16	10	4	2	62	47	0.00	257.00
Lancashire	16	6	2	8	64	43	0.00	223.00
Surrey	16	6	3	7	63	44	0.00	219.00
Kent	16	6	5	5	47	47	0.00	198.00
Warwickshire	16	4	5	7*	50	37	2.50	171.50
Middlesex	16	3	3	10	46	41	0.00	169.00
Essex	16	3	5	8*	34	45	0.00	156.00
Nottinghamshire	16	2	8	6	36	45	1.00	132.00
Leicestershire	16	1	6	9	36	40	0.50	125.50

*includes one tied match

AVERAGES 2003

BATTING

	M	Inns	N.O.	Runs	Hs	Avge	SR
M.W. Goodwin	16	28	3	1,496	335*	59.84	63.68
M.J. Prior	16	24	3	1,006	153*	47.90	74.96
P.A. Cottey	15	25	0	1,149	188	45.96	52.06
T.R. Ambrose	15	26	3	931	93*	40.47	48.38
M.H. Yardy	2	3	0	116	69	38.66	32.31
R.S.C. Martin-Jenkins	16	25	3	811	121*	36.86	66.20
C.J. Adams	16	27	0	966	190	35.77	63.51
R.J. Kirtley	11	13	7	207	40*	34.50	37.70
R.R. Montgomerie	16	28	2	884	107	34.00	46.97
Mushtaq Ahmed	16	19	2	456	60	26.82	81.42
M.J.G. Davis	10	12	2	258	168	25.90	41.24
K.J. Innes	7	11	3	182	103*	22.75	45.61
B.V. Taylor	7	7	4	55	35*	18.33	23.60
J.D. Lewry	11	15	3	215	70	17.91	87.04
P.M. Hutchison	3	3	0	23	18	7.66	26.13

CENTURIES

M.W. Goodwin (4)	335*	v.	Leicestershire (Hove)
	210	v.	Essex (Colchester)
	148	v.	Nottinghamshire (Trent Bridge)
	118*	v.	Lancashire (Old Trafford)
M.J. Prior (4)	153*	v.	Essex (Colchester)
	148	v.	Middlesex (Hove)
	133	v.	Nottinghamshire (Horsham)
	100	v.	Warwickshire (Hove)
C.J. Adams (4)	140 and 190	v.	Lancashire (Hove)
	107	v.	Surrey (Hove)
	102	v.	Leicestershire (Hove)

P.A. Cottey (3)   188 v. Warwickshire (Hove)
                          147 v. Leicestershire (Leicester)
                          107 v. Essex (Arundel)
R.R. Montgomerie   105 v. Nottinghamshire (Horsham)
R.S.C. Martin-Jenkins   121* v. Nottinghamshire (Trent Bridge)
M.J.G. Davis   168 v. Middlesex (Hove)
K.J. Innes   103* v. Nottinghamshire (Horsham)

HALF-CENTURIES

T.R. Ambrose (9)   88 and 93 v. Essex (Arundel)
                          85   v. Warwickshire (Edgbaston)
                          82   v. Leicestershire (Hove)
                          76* v. Surrey (Hove)
                          75   v. Surrey (Oval)
                          55   v. Nottinghamshire (Horsham)
                          51   v. Middlesex (Lord's)
                          50   v. Warwickshire (Hove)
P.A. Cottey (7)   98   v. Essex (Arundel)
                          58   v. Nottinghamshire (Horsham)
                          58   v. Leicestershire (Leicester)
                          56   v. Leicestershire (Hove)
                          55   v. Warwickshire (Edgbaston)
                          53   v. Nottinghamshire (Horsham)
                          52   v. Kent (Tunbridge Wells)
R.R. Montgomerie (7)   97   v. Essex (Colchester)
                          90   v. Surrey (Hove)
                          72 and 70 v. Lancashire (Hove)
                          66   v. Warwickshire (Hove)
                          54* v. Middlesex (Hove)
                          52   v. Leicestershire (Leicester)
M.W. Goodwin (5)   96   v. Kent (Hove)
                          75   v. Surrey (Hove)
                          60   v. Surrey (Oval)
                          58   v. Kent (Tunbridge Wells)
                          57   v. Lancashire (Old Trafford)
R.S.C. Martin-Jenkins (5) 61 and 88 v. Surrey (Oval)
                          67 and 84 v. Kent (Tunbridge Wells)
                          50   v. Middlesex (Lord's)
M.J. Prior (3)   96   v. Leicestershire (Leicester)
                          84   v. Warwickshire (Edgbaston)
                          50* v. Surrey (Hove)
Mushtaq Ahmed (3)   60   v. Lancashire (Hove)
                          57   v. Middlesex (Hove)
                          54   v. Lancashire (Old Trafford)
C.J. Adams (2)   62   v. Kent (Tunbridge Wells)
                          54   v. Kent (Hove)
J.D. Lewry (1)   70   v. Essex (Colchester)
M.H. Yardy (1)   69   v. Surrey (Oval)

BOWLING

	O	M	R	W	Avge	SR	Econ
R.R. Montgomerie	3	0	9	1	9.00	18.0	3.00
Mushtaq Ahmed	836.3	163	2,539	103	24.65	48.7	3.03
J.D. Lewry	315.2	71	1,020	41	24.87	46.1	3.23
R.J. Kirtley	430.2	95	1,403	49	28.63	52.6	3.26
B.V. Taylor	214.1	60	617	21	29.38	61.1	2.88
R.S.C. M.-Jenkins	364	82	1,258	31	40.58	70.4	3.45
K.J. Innes	64	11	297	7	42.43	63.4	4.01
M.J.G. Davis	220	42	703	14	50.21	94.2	3.19
P.M. Hutchison	77	12	311	3	103.66	154.0	4.03
C.J. Adams	1	0	1	0	-	-	1.00
M.W. Goodwin	3	0	17	0	-	-	5.66
P.A. Cottey	13	1	59	0	-	-	4.53
M.H. Yardy	27	3	89	0	-	-	3.29

FIVE-WICKET HAULS

Mushtaq Ahmed (10)	32.4-9-85-7	v. Warwickshire (Hove)
	48-7-157-6	v. Warwickshire (Edgbaston)
	7.1-3-163-6 & 30-9-81-6	v. Nottinghamshire (Horsham)
	33-4-93-5 & 17.2-3-70-5	v. Kent (Tunbridge Wells)
	41.5.-18-96-5	v. Leicestershire (Leicester)
	48-10-124-6 & 33.2-14-49-5	v. Lancashire (Hove)
	40-4-145-6	v. Middlesex (Hove)
J.D. Lewry (3)	24.1-3-106-8	v. Leicestershire (Hove)
	29-7-72-5 & 19.4.-6-52-5	v. Essex (Arundel)
R.J. Kirtley (2)	15-4-26-6	v. Kent (Hove)
	23-9-60-5	v. Nottinghamshire (Trent Bridge)

FIELDING

36	T.R. Ambrose (29ct,7st)
28	M.J. Prior
22	R.R. Montgomerie
18	C.J. Adams
10	M.W. Goodwin
8	P.A. Cottey
7	R.S.C. Martin-Jenkins
4	J.D. Lewry
4	M.J.G. Davis
3	M.H. Yardy
3	Mushtaq Ahmed
3	R.J. Kirtley
1	K.J. Innes

Ambrose kept wicket in ten matches, Prior in six.

Other sports titles published by Tempus

Sussex CCC

JOHN WALLACE

This selection of over 220 images includes fascinating photographs and memorablia that illustrate the team's history, from the middle of the nineteenth century up to the start of the twenty-first. Particular attention has been given to the strong family connection within the club, to the great players, such as John Langridge, Ted Dexter, Jim Parks and Tony Greig, and to the grounds on which they played.
0 7524 2192 1

Sussex CCC Greats

JOHN WALLACE

As cricket enters the twenty-first century, with its multitude of changes and initiatives, it seems appropriate to celebrate the lives of some of the men who have been part and parcel of the history of Sussex, the oldest of the county cricket clubs in this country. Since its formation in 1839, many Sussex players have brought great distinction to the game, on and off the field.
0 7524 2421 1

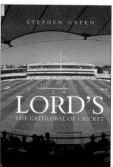

Sussex CCC Classics

JOHN WALLACE

Sussex County Cricket Club, the oldest of the county clubs, have been playing cricket since time immemorial, although trophies have been relatively few and far between. For all that, classic matches certainly do abound. John Wallace recounts some of the most memorable matches which Sussex have played.
0 7524 2739 9

Lord's Cathedral of Cricket

STEPHEN GREEN

The history of the greatest and most evocative sports ground in the world. *Lord's: The Cathedral of Cricket*, charts the history of the ground from its foundation by Thomas Lord in 1787 through to the twenty-first century stadium with its state-of-the-art media centre. Exciting matches and great events are brought to life in this remarkable book by former museum curator and MCC librarian, Stephen Green.
0 7524 2167 0

If you are interested in purchasing other books published by Tempus, or in case you have difficulty finding any Tempus books in your local bookshop, you can also place orders directly through our website

www.tempus-publishing.com

or from **BOOKPOST**, Freepost, PO Box 29, Douglas, Isle of Man, IM99 1BQ
tel 01624 836000   email bookshop@enterprise.net